MIDNIGHT
STROLL

MIDNIGHT STROLL

JANICE KULYK KEEFER

Exile Editions

Ҽ

30 YEARS OF PUBLISHING

1976 - 2006

Library and Archives Canada Cataloguing in Publication

Keefer, Janice Kulyk, 1952-

  Midnight stroll / Janice Kulyk Keefer.

Poems, with paintings, monoprints and drawings, and photographs by
Natalka Husar, Claire Weissman Wilks and Goran Petkovsky.

ISBN 1-55096-070-9

  I. Husar, Natalka, 1951- II. Wilks, Claire Weissman, 1933-
III. Petkovski, Goran IV. Title.

PS8571.E435M53 2006   C811'.54   C2006-905891-1

Design and Composition by Homunculus ReproSet
Typeset in Birka and Bembo at the Moons of Jupiter Studios
Printed in Canada by Gauvin Imprimerie

The publisher would like to acknowledge the financial assistance of
The Canada Council for the Arts and the Ontario Arts Council.

Conseil des Arts du Canada   Canada Council for the Arts

ONTARIO ARTS COUNCIL
CONSEIL DES ARTS DE L'ONTARIO

First published in Canada in 2006 by Exile Editions Ltd.
144483 Southgate Road 14
General Delivery
Holstein, Ontario, N0G 2A0
info@exileeditions.com
www.ExileEditions.com

Canadian Sales Distribution: U.S. Sales Distribution:
McArthur & Company   Independent Publishers Group
c/o Harper Collins   814 North Franklin Street
1995 Markham Road   Chicago, IL 60610
Toronto, ON M1B 5M8   www.ipgbook.com
toll free: 1 800 387 0117   toll free: 1 800 888 4741

for
Connie Rooke

Reading

for Connie

A garden, summer, a river,

a woman. She is not on a swing,
or crumpling her silks on the grass:
she is in a hammock, and she is reading.

The web holds her, the arms of the trees,
the silver bracelet on her arm: sun
sways in the water below her.

This air holds something golden;
it honeys the leaves
in their dark clusters. The nymph

forever emptying her urn
which is forever full, hears it:
a hum, the deep murmur
between eyes and page.

Think of the paintings of women, reading.
Magdalens, mistresses, letter-lovers.
How the paper in their hands

turns lucent as pearls, drinking
the gleam of ink. How they lean
into language, as if they were sails
on windy seas, these women, reading.

Her husband, wading among the watercress
does not call out to her, knowing
her mind holds the book the way the hammock
holds, but does not enclose her,

this woman in whom
there is the warmth of coral
worn against skin; whose arms
always open in greeting.

One rare summer afternoon:
a book, her only intimate. The stillness
in this garden is an instrument, put softly down;
light across the water weaves
its burning nets—

nothing disturbs
these words, travelling
the blue roads of her eyes.

I

Midnight Stroll

after paintings
by
Natalka Husar

Mississauga Mama Meets the Artist Who Knows Too Much

Cyclone *semblables*: whirling
till I'm dizzier than Doris McCarthy siamesed
with Doris Day. I can hardly hold my brush, my shopping bag
straight. Either way, I'm long past innocence, technical
or sexual. I know my paints the way I've learned
my skin, all swathes and swags, mottlings,
dimples, stretchmarks. I know
what paint and love can
and can't do.

In the end, it all comes down to
carpets & curtains: earth and air.
Fur? It's in-between: rug
you roll up in, drapery
for bared shoulders. Dead pelt of a dead
animal, become our second, wiser skin. Disguise
for flesh fallen for the villain: sag. Don't
get me wrong, there's nothing more paintable
(Rubens, Rembrandt, Lucian Freud) but half of me
is happier quoting Clinique: *Anti-Gravity
Firming Lift Cream.*

The other half is after—what else—Truth!
Of material object, of atmosphere's effect
on material object, the way light
daggers the diagonal of strung bedsheet;
escorts a length of lace to black's back
guillotine. Possession, re-
production of material object, caught on canvas
or in canvas shopping bag.

Once I was Empress
of Immaculate Conceptions, floor-length mink madonna.
My shoes were spiked, lipstick
wouldn't melt on my teeth, holy
husband I held up like the UnterChrist in jewel-
gloved hands. Self-parody, self-portrait—even this
grey ghost projected on a padlocked door. Now
dinner's done, guests gone, and Cinderella
sings the blues to rumpled sheets
and tacked-up linen: flytraps for images she can't command,

a whole baby carriage full, plus hangers-on. No mother
could have named them better, drawn them
more exact. *I don't paint anything I don't see:*
Amendment, *I don't paint anything that doesn't*
give me the creeps. Paying acute attention—
never call it loving: love's a music,
not a witness-box.

No rag and bone shop where my ladders start.
A kitchen, bedroom, studio:
an unmade head. I take up my brush—take up,
hurl down, chisel, scrape away,
compelled to paint just
what I see: milky way in a roasting pan, true
romance's polyester sheen, whole libraries
of nightmare dolled-up
in desire's flesh-tones,

against

the all and only: light
and dark:
black and white.

Midnight Stroll

Bumper crop of babies: out of room
on the orphanage express. Are those bows
or bandages in your hair? Where are you
going? Who
is taking you there? Our Lady in Blue:
gloved and grinning,
heels spiking
the pavement that isn't there.

Scowling, sulking, finger-sucking:
is this any way to treat a getaway?
How about Cuba's sunny sands, ideal
for balding children nursing tumours
instead of dolls. Surely you're big enough
to get there on your own two feet,
if you could trust the dark
to bear you up.

Black buggy; black ground.
If this is midnight,
don't count on reaching morning. Better
to dream yourselves away, each face
a cameo-balloon unsnipped
from any string but
the wires pinching tighter
and tighter
holes
through your ears.

Horseshoes and Waves

This half-shaved head: not surgery—
coquetterie. My finger's a cigarette
I'm taking one long, cool drag on.
If this pose won't do, teach me another

Hypocrite Voyeur,
my mirror, my
mother.

Changing Spots

Party time chez Our Lord and Lady
of Mississauga! Top-drawer guests
parade their mink,
their leopard and their ocelot;

toss them
in the Master Bedroom's
Persian-carpet cage,
where the hired help hangs out
once dinner's served.

(The girls' English is bad
but they smile a lot.)

Under the rug, the ghost
of another rug. Under the borrowed fur,
skin's pale lining.

Cinderella in Mink

Works in any language. All you need:
barenaked skin, and a prince
with a shoe fetish. You're wearing
his driving gloves, and his mama's mink,
the one they couldn't bring themselves
to take to Value Village when she shuffled off.
It looks good on you—it suits
your tallow-sculpted shoulders, even
the lipstick check mark above your eye.

In Grimm, the sisters hacked off their toes
for a perfect fit. Somewhere, dark-browed maidens
croon in moonlight for their cossack prince, but
you clued in
long time ago. No cherry bloom for you.
No wreaths or ballgowns, just
nakedness,
a cloudy smile

and all those blood-stuffed shoes.

Cinderella After Midnight

This is how it goes: a cigarette,
a cellphone, a feather bed that makes you think
of sugar-powdered waffles. You have to explain 'waffles'
to the folks back home. Now's a good time to call:
sunrise over Donetsk, though Mama's
flat's in constant shadow.

If she could see you now. If they could all
just see you, swaddled in mink
on a red velvet pillow. Your underpants
still fit, and your legs stretch long as the limbs
of a birch—tell that one to Mama. Tell her
how the wife's off at the cottage with the kids
and there's no one left to make trouble here.
Tell her you've been offered
a holiday in Istanbul, all expenses paid
and shop till you drop. But you won't—

drop, that is.
You're headed up and away!
Nothing can stop you, not even
those too-tight shoes
on the feet you no longer feel.

Imitation Marriage

Champagne-bubble-blonde
(vintage Crimean, extra-fruity)
desires to meet Canadian Businessman
(2 cars, cottage. Wife and kids optional)
for regular rendezvous. No strings attached,
no promises necessary, just
the goods, on demand. Weekend getaways
to Niagara Falls, or better yet,

Buffalo (the shopping's better). Cellphone
and shoes, the odd sexy
bra or sweater, working up
to the kiss-off: mink.
Plus anything you can spare for the Homeland
(my two younger sisters;
my brother who has to get to university).

Imitation divorce
guaranteed.

1231

A HUSAR 1999 ROMANCE

50¢

IMITATION MARRIAGE

R

1783

A HUSAR 1999 ROMANCE

60c

CINDERELLA IN MINK

373-01783-060

1075

A HUSAR 2001 ROMANCE

45c

Cinderella
After Midnight

1052

1052

A HUSAR 2001 ROMANCE

45¢

MEANT FOR EACH OTHER

MEANT FOR EACH OTHER · MARY BURCHELL

R

Never Call It Loving

Bohdan—Bobo for short. Lawyer by day,
lover by night. All those dinner meetings,
late night conferences when you step into fantasy's
phone booth, step out superhero-costumed:
baby blue boxers flecked with cinammon hearts.

Who can resist you, Bobo? Not your bubble-
blonde from Poltava. She's been dreaming
of sweeter-than-sugar-beet you since she's been old enough
to keep her dreams a secret. Hands-on-hips,
or tucked into your briefs' strained elastic, as you threaten

belly laughs or bonking. Uncorked,
the champagne broods in its narrow jail;
passion-purple curtains offer fold
after fold for her to count all night.

Two Paths

Old county girls,
specialists
in surviving meltdowns: Varka
and Darka, though they'll soon be Barb
and Donna. Girls from another planet,
girls from the Dead Zone, the Dead-Enders.

Their big sisters list with *Ukrainian Girls International*
'interested in sincere friendship and everlasting
marriage.' Their mothers' hearts are flat
as their feet: lifelong queues for milk and meat.
Kid brothers steal cars by day; guard cars
all night in lock-up lots, playing 2-handed poker
with pistols on the tables. Fathers? They
cut out long ago: desertion, disappearance,
death-by-vodka.

Darka's a home help for the elderly
in Bloor West Village. Varka works under
several tables in jobs you don't need
a uniform for. They share a basement apartment
off Dundas and dream Mississauga; they shop
Biway and send home photos snapped
in front of fountains at the shopping mall.

In this place, even the sky is blonde
and ghosts throw no shadows.

The Garden of Dreams

I am your guide, your muse and mentor.
My cold hand claims you, like a mercury filling,
like an ink stain. I'm paint
on a blackboard; you could learn
me like a multiplication table, plug me
into a socket to glow through the night. My flesh
is ample; better feast than famine. You will learn,
little fair one, you will learn.

The sky is black; against it your hair glows,
will-o'-the-wisp to northern lights. You play
Cranach's Eve, hatless, tilted, mink tails
in place of golden chains. Me,
I'm Ingres' Madame Moitessier, unseated,
stripped to her slip.

The price is right, the garden empty, dreams
don't pay the rent. Whatever
you thought you'd unearthed here
is unearthly: limelight
picks us both out of the dark, holds us
by our hair, then
lets us drop.

Strangers May Marry

so why shouldn't lovers do the cheek-
to-cheek? My black-eyed, black-browed poet
fresh from the wilds of *Hutsulshchyna*: never seen,
never worn a dinner jacket before.

What hubby wants, I want, ten times over.
Barrettes and ponytails, my hair still smelling
of fresh bread. The blindness of that blonde
on his miracle-fibre knees.

Stardisco behind us, goosebumps
on night's skin. Sweetheart, *sertseh,*
are you dancing or drowning? Your hand,
is it waving Hi or Bye-Bye?

Don't think I can't read
your kind of verse, don't think
I'll ever let you go

my lion, my Byron, my
Bohuslav-call-me-Brian:
ghostly bolster in my bed of dreams.

The Wide Fields of Home

Sleep, baby, sleep. God knows
where your daddy is: not here,
thank God. My lap's big enough
for you yet.

Lucky you, out like
you'd been hit by a truck.
Lucky me. I glow grey
not green, sucking honey
from cigarette straws.

Sleep on, sleep awhile,
till the ash burns down,
little rag doll daughter,
little rag doll me.

Meant for Each Other

Another day, another night, another
blondchik. Older, this time
your eyes both downcast
and come-hither.

He only has eyes for you, now,
he's even stripped off his wristwatch
though he can't let the glasses go.
The better to see you with, my
dear Lady of Mississauga can keep his dinner
in the microwave all night, for all he cares.
He's got you, girl, and you've

got that high-stepping, shoulder-padded,
fox-fur jacket you're fingering
with your hand outspread, thumb
red from where you've sucked it raw
(bad-baby habits die so hard).

No hurt intended, not a touch
of harm. That poison you breathed
through the green rain of childhood
he will neutralize with every flub-a-dub
of his hamsteak thighs

while you make eyes
at the VISA in his wallet;
his gold-skinned house of cards.

Beloved Enemy

Whatever passion spent, they lie
together in the King-Size bed, Ramada Inn
(anybody's guess which city, country). She wears
the wife's 15th-anniversary diamond pendant
and bracelet, or facsimile thereof. Her nightie
conjuring the blue of Caribbean seas, she stares

at the cancelled boyfriend back in Zhytomyr,
her absent mother, the teenaged daughter
she'll be saddled with in fifteen years. The way she lays
her jewelled hand upon his chest: *gold
in them thar hills!* in spite
of his idiot grin and fogged-up
spectacles, his face blank
as his mid-range wristwatch.

In summer dark, cossack whispers
to maiden: *come, dear one,
into the orchard. The stars are so bright
you could find a pin in the grass.*

Bright as your bouffant, over
the obstinate, unsecret dark
rooting your hair.

The Golden Madonna

Gold as in Clairol, not karats, this
time round. Her parka quotes
the Virgin's colours: white
and Black Sea blue. In a pink
fleece suit her baby toddles
on the moon of mama's breast.

Joseph? He's shovelling snow
in Etobicoke. The Holy Ghost's
at the mall's white sale, and God's off

golfing in Florida.

A HUSAR 2001 ROMANCE

THE GOLDEN MADONNA

MIDNIGHT STROLL

Paintings ~ *Natalka Husar*

• in order of appearance •

Changing Spots, 1999, oil on linen, 221cm x 142cm

Imitation Marriage, 1999, oil on book cover, 17cm x 11cm

Cinderella in Mink, 1999, oil on book cover, 17cm x 11cm

Cinderella After Midnight, 2001, oil on book cover, 17cm x 11cm

Meant for Each Other, 2001, oil on book cover, 17cm x 11cm

The Golden Madonna, 2001, oil on book cover, 17cm x 11cm

Horseshoes and Waves, 2001, oil on linen, 218cm x 142cm

II

Etty Hillesum

1914–1943

for

Claire Weissman Wilks

Let the stars of its dawn be dark;
let it hope for light, but have none, nor see the eyelids of the morning.

Job 3:9

Hineinhorchen

Italicized passages used in the poems are quotations and close readings

drawn from *Etty: The Letters and Diaries of Etty Hillesum 1941-1943*.

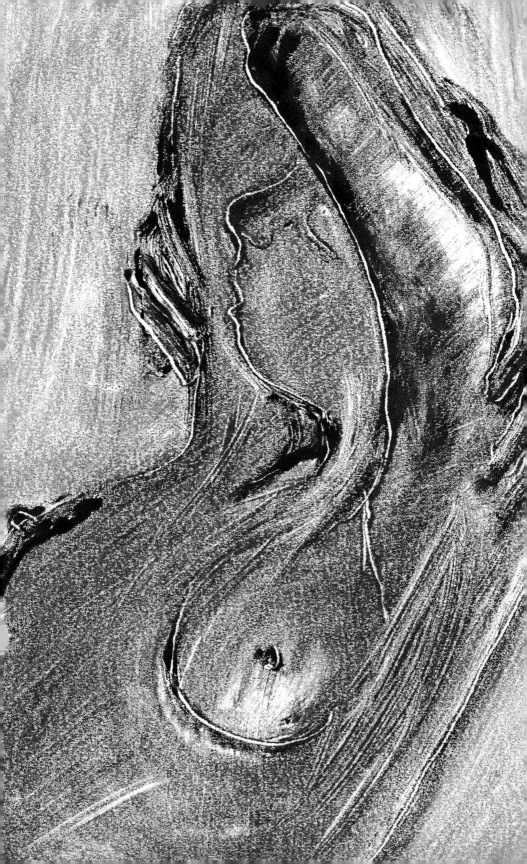

ONE

Amsterdam

*I would be happy washing dishes
for a living, as long as I had a field
of study of my own.*

Circumstances

War, the Second World.
As if there haven't been hundreds
before: ask the Carthaginians,
the Aztecs, ask the Neanderthals
—as many wars as there are worlds.

Amsterdam, during the Second World War.
Occupation: resistance.
Executions: screams across the heath;
strangled interrogations.

A Jew, in Amsterdam, during the Second World War.
Roaring trade in yellow cloth, earthbound
constellations. Rationing, registrations,
round-ups.

A Jewish woman in Amsterdam during the Second World War.
Age, 27. Unmarried, childless, no occupation
in particular. A law degree, a love
of Rilke and Russian; a view
out a window at Gabrielmetsustraat, 6
(the Rijksmuseum flanked by trees).
Heart unencumbered, soul
one block of black granite.

Portrait of the Writer as an Old Soul

A Turkish rug for a curtain.
On the wall, a fierce Moroccan girl—a photo,
torn from a magazine. On my desk
a typewriter, cigarettes, this exercise book,
this little coat hanger *from which*
a whole evening—a single hour—
hangs

No lady at window:
no letter, no spinnet,

no pearls.

Sinnbild

Each waking
a birth from night's warm belly.

Chill of a damp, grey day:
a bright shawl over my terracotta-coloured sweater.

Queues for butter, queues for bread.
That bolt of gypsy cloth I saved.

Yellow stars, regulation height, width, stitch.
A dress *open on all sides to the sun, the wind and his caresses.*

Forbidden trains, trams, bicycles.
A whole summer on the heath,

me in the gysy dress with tanned,
bare legs and flowing gypsy hair

and then a small farmhouse with a low-beamed ceiling
and the smell of apples, and a view over the heath at night.

Through ocean's grey eternity,
my narrow boat.

Birth of an Uncarried Child

Ten days since I first knew
you were alive.

At fourteen I went to watch
my mother at the asylum. You could
not call it visiting. My brothers
checked themselves in and out of the ward
as if it were a hotel:
big spenders.

Käthe, who weeps
over what's become of her *Heimat*
warms the towels, scalds water, secures
quinine. You gush

into this madness
innocent of flag or star
or life.

Wrestling Match with Julius

Integral Part of the Treatment:
analyst, analysand getting down to basics
(viz. the floor: bare, unswept).

Playfully, at first, and then to win.
Massive man, mere woman
(half his age, his bulk)

I floored him, then
dabbed his split lip with cologne. I,

orderer of chaos, reclaimer of land
from raging seas, dauntless
darner of stockings,

more than a match for a balding, half-deaf
refugee: more wisdom
in one of his eyebrow hairs
than in whole libraries.

Unleashing, in that clumsy dust and sweat
that final, liberating scream
that always sticks bashfully in your throat
when you make love.

Daily Round

Wake, wash, write.

Prepare breakfast for the household
with Käthe's help

(Käthe, our German cook,
teaches me how to make mock
whipped cream.)

Return to my room to study Old Slavonic.
Lunch.
Teach Russian to my merchant from
Enkhuizen, who brings us sacks of gold
disguised as beans. Teach Russian
to that bold young woman
with the sleek head of a boy.

Cross 5 streets, 1 bridge
and 2 canals to Courbetstraat.
Transcribe his shorthand notes:
all the cries and cramps
of the souls he cares for.

A little wrestling, a little nestling
then home to peel vegetables for supper.
Reading by the stove, or out
to our only concert halls:
our friends' cramped parlours.

Home, bath, book—perhaps
the telephone, his voice through the wire
close enough to stroke my throat.

To bed with Han, or better,
the narrowness of my solitary cot. Shedding
the day with my clothes, diving clean
into dark.

Our Common Fate

Everyone who seeks to save himself
must surely realize that if he does not go,
another must take his place.
As if it mattered which of us goes.

To harass, to humiliate,
beat and break us. To plunder,
enslave, strip us bare. But

to annihilate? Each one of us,
senile and foetal,
parent and child.

I will not hide myself
like a rat in a wall. I refuse
a job's short safety,
selling my people in job lots.

Let others launch their leaky rafts.
I will join all those
on their backs, in this vast
sea, staring up at the sky

going down with prayer
on their lips

My naked feet
on iron ground

their lips.

Palm Reader

Julius, you ladies' man, you troll, you
bluff, big-bellied, *biscuit-loving uncle,*
50-year-old clod of earth.
Roman Emperor or mere Olympian?
Sultan whose passions swell the curve
of your lower lip, the right-hand corner.

God-seeker, God-giver, teacher
of the act and need of prayer.
Sitting with you at the dinner table,
your face washed with moonlight, young
as a crocus.

You have only to stretch out your arms
for women's breasts to home to your hands.
The heavy fullness of your mouth, suppleness
of tongue. Confiding
that you never masturbate after
saying your prayers; lecturing me
on the precise function of the clitoris.

I never worshipped you: you
invaded me. In spite of your pale and faraway,
your sad, saved fiancée, I was intent
we should marry, just
to face Poland, together.

Even that longing fell from me.
I no longer desired you, but knew you. Not
the false teeth, hearing aid,
the way you sing, *like an old lion who's
stepped on a razor blade,*

but the grey landscape
of your face, the tired lakes of your eyes,
older than I will ever be:

the greatest
and deepest happiness of my life
sipping your breath
from the beaker of your mouth.

Alchemy

To belong to one's experience. And to transform it.

Turning shit to gold. Jackboots
to bare & blistered feet.

To make the vulnerable
strong, to give the beaten
the ultimate
and only form of power:

to forgive.

Life

I am not I, there is nothing
to which I need put my name.

Nothing to do or say to show
I am worthy to have lived.

I need know nothing, understand
nothing.

At my feet, a feather:
Eternity.

With Liesl at the Dressmaker's

small bird,
        moonlight bather on warm
          summer nights

yet strong enough to clean
spinach 3 hours each day;
queue another 3 for bread.

Two young children, a husband
whose hand running down my face
is the claw of a bird of prey.

I draw you to me in my sleep,
wake in a shudder of flesh.

Lover I will never lie with,
my only girlfriend,
small Liesl
who will outlive us all.

A Vast and Fruitful Loneliness

I love to be alone so much. And...
we Jews are being crowded
into ever smaller spaces.

All the roads inside me, the endless
highways, the gates You unlocked—
How much space there was for me.

Plain, heath, so easily crossed:
soul's native land, the vast
horizons of one's whole life,
only just
opening.

Inside me a rapacious sea
and the fistful of land I've reclaimed.

Just before waking, I feel, inside me
spaces and distances locked up
wanting to break out, to unfold
into ever wider spaces and distances

feel them like the necks of horses
stamping and pawing in a crowded stable

infinite steppes spread out inside me:
their wind on my face, their earth.

Ascetic

I study
how to be hungry. How
to be cold, dirty, a prey to lice.
How to unlearn comfort. Comfort takes
too much energy; mourning its loss
takes too much time.

I practice nakedness,
disrobing myself of the day, entering night
the way one slips into a bath, needing
and having nothing.

Day's dirt and fears: something
to let drop, subject
to the gravity of these times.

I am learning to remember
hyacinth-scented soap, cashmere or
crèpe de chine against my skin.

Each new day, a garment
so rich, so unexpected
I cannot tell whether to tug it
over my head, or
inch inside.

Jasmine, from the Balcony

So radiant, so virginal.
An exuberant young bride lost
in a back street.

Do not grieve that you cannot take in
the beauty of jasmine. No need.
Miracles cancel the need for belief.

Soon lice will be eating us up in Poland;
storms will bruise the jasmine—drowned shreds
in mud-pools on the garage roof—

while somewhere inside me
jasmine will bloom undisturbed,
profuse, delicate. That jasmine:

it has been there
a long time—but only now
are words beginning to fail me
about it.

Room

Beloved stove, grey day,
whimpering stomach, woollen dress,
slim, strong hand.

My everywhere: my desert island,
convent cell with a view
onto anything I wish to see:
cornfields or a caliph's palace.

Crammed bookcase: one huge, layered mind.
Desk: my true half, my trusty bicycle's
second self.

I carry you inside me on streets I walk
till my heels run blood. I will keep you
in barracks crammed
with plank beds, matchstick bodies.

Each morning, one
silent hour here: six minutes
or sixty. Foundation of all that follows:

If I don't work every moment,
make use of this time with all
my energy and concentration

I will have lived even less
than what's been granted me.

Between Sleep and Waking

a moment when all heaviness falls away,
when life is so indescribably
good and light to bear that it seems
sheer surface—a glittering, bright
wide plain.

Sheer surface exists no more than peace.
I know this: there are
caves and caverns, too,
though to describe them so
turns them into something out of
fairy tales, or Mendelsohn.

Caves are cold, deep, dank,
dark. You cannot see to read;
you cannot move to write.

The night they issued the decree
(for our heads heaped on platters)
we sat on comfortable chairs
(bought with insurance money against bomb damage).

Philosophising together, drinking real coffee,
we could not have been happier.
Cave dwellers. Skaters.

Sun Lounge

In a northern country known
for brisk winds, this
ripe pleasure:
sun full on my face, my bare feet,
as I talk with friends, breaking
the bread of the day.

Confirmed voluptuary,
seasoned lover,
bosom-shaking dancer,

abandoned ascetic.
Fiery marrow, fleshy
bones.

In the Ice-Cream Parlour

Wall-to-wall yellow. Sunlight trapped
in cream. We sit and eat,

having just signed
(polite, with smiles)
our death-warrants, in the Gestapo Hall.

This place is cosy as the cloth
from which we cut our stars, the warm coats
to which we stitch them.

Useless,
imagining the kind of dark
they'll light, one day.
Why turn sugar-cream
to wax and ashes?

Sufficient unto each day
the evil thereof.

Vanilla, chocolate, licorice.

Rumours and Reports

One must not die while still alive,
One has to live one's life to the full
And to the end.

Mind stumbles to the door they're beating;
listens carefully, keeps them
off the threshold. Body

betrays, lets them in to shit on the rug,
torch the beams or hack them
into a thousand splinters: *each piece*
has a different pain.

If they are true, we can do nothing.
If false, they're strong enough
to poison sleep.

There will always be suffering—
What difference whether from this or that?

Leave us at least the little hope
we have left, the little time.

But when they call up
girls of sixteen, when the whole
earth becomes one prison camp.
When the Germans—so the story goes—
bury us alive or kill us with gas

leave us, at least, some small grace
in suffering.

Time

In two years,
from minute to minute,
you can live a long life.

Reading Rilke, St Augustine.
Queuing, by starlight, for the belief

that even in the last moment
of the most terrible death,
life has been good.

From heartbeat to heartbeat:
immersion in this now, this here. Still,

there's Russia, there's heaven:
distant horizons that lie
beyond these days.

Telephone

Each time you call, Beloved—
an adventure.

Who knew how Bacchic
that stern, black instrument could be?

Wires so sensitive they fingerprint
the thrum of a throat.

A different voice, a different ring
in the daytime, than in the evening:

before I pick it up, I always know
whether it's life, or death.

Too Much Reality

A poem by Rilke is real and as important
as a young man falling out of an airplane.
All that happens, happens in this world of ours
and you must not leave one thing out
for the sake of another.

So let us be jugglers, God.
Ambidextrous
Siamese twins, alchemists
turning earth to air, blood
to something clearer than water;

granite
to flesh, and flesh to prayer,

a cheese coupon
into one line from *The Book of Hours*.

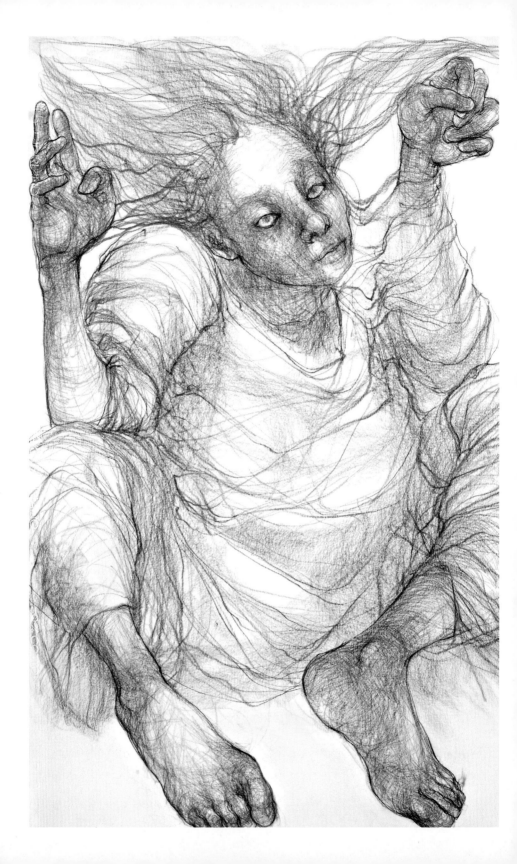

Hineinhorchen

That German for which, again,
there's no Dutch word.

Laying your ear
against your own breast,

not thinking:
inlistening—

sensing the slow, dark ripening:
soul's free and full surrender.

The pause between two breaths
hearkens unto itself, and unto others,

unto God, the spirit
in me, God
to God.

Stadionkade

My wrung-out belly,
bandaged
by a hot water bottle. Chilblains
gouging my feet;
a woollen shawl on my clotted head.

All the better to see you with, my dear,
dear steppes of the Skating Club grounds:
stripped, snow-blind.

On your sands we walked and walked,
discussing poetry, he with a tin of condensed milk
bought in a perfume shop, I
with a bag of golden rennet apples.

Such swag! Such boundlessness!
Carrying milk and apples,
knowing, suddenly,
that beyond this, there is
nothing more. What is,

the vastness of what is. Then,
nothing.

The Patient

(From *patior*: Latin, deponent verb.
Meaning: 'I suffer' or 'it is suffered by me.')

Ills of the Body
Leaden fatigue.
Headache, restlessness,
severe menstrual pains.
Erotic greed.

Ills of the Mind
Stone-sadness, anxiety, fear:
(madness in the family: schizophrenia,
to be doctrinaire).

Ills of the Heart
A coward, a dullard who has yet
to make a friend of any stranger, to give
an Other root-room in a heart
that's no mere
flower pot.

Ills of the Soul
Spiritual constipation, civil
war between head and heart. Waste,
chaos: self a mere bag of
spikes, shards.
Shame.

Cure
Unclench, one by one
soul's small, stiff fingers. Dig
the way diviners do. Through dirt to liquid
crystal.

        • • •

Uncover your gift, what
you will do with your life.
Help others, clouded, shattered
as you are, to that honesty called clarity.

Speak and write words
of fired ice, their truth close
as leaves pressed against
a window.

Become complete, whole, a
human being. No fear
of really being nothing but
a ridiculous amateur.

Self & Others

If I don't start with myself,
how can I change anything for the better?
If I don't know myself,
how can I understand others

just as confused and weak, just
as helpless as me? Even that young
Gestapo officer shouting at me
had more need of my compassion
than I of his.

It is not in my nature *to hate*
any human being for his so-called wickedness.
Injustice, suffering
move me to pity, not rage (though
I denounce with the best and worst).

A little peace, a lot of kindness,
and a little wisdom.

Prayer

I.

Sitting on the dustbin
on the small, stony terrace.
Hidden, head leaning
against the washtub, sun stoking
my black hair, my white eyelids.

The map my mind draws, from the bare
branches of the chestnut, to the rasp
of sparrows. Tracing all angles and objects,
reading each furrow of tree bark, until something

(more and less
than that push
from my mother's salt sea)

occurs in me, occurs,
deep down. As a child
taking up her first crayon, draws
not this or that
but colour itself, in
and as
itself.

II.

Eyes cast down, not heavenwards.
Pretending, when someone walks by,
to look for a button burst from a coat.

The girl who learned to pray,
forced to her knees by something
stronger, better than herself:

by the doors blown off
the chaos within.

III.

Uncork this bottle,
shame-stoppered.
Embed this gesture
into bone and flesh.

My bone,
my flesh.

Between bed and bookcase,
room enough to bend, knees clasping floor,
fingers interlaced: strong shoots:
willow or the rushes splayed
across the bottom of the broken chair.

My body's laws of gravity and need:
lead weights, to make drapes hang true.
Jewels sewn in the seams of a refugee's coat.

Holding the book of my face, my hands.
Closer than any nakedness
before a new lover:

prayer threading the maze to my self
and You.

At the Pharmacy

Where, trying to buy toothpaste,
I am grilled by *someone in the shape*
of a fellow human being.

"Are you permitted to—?" the word, *Jew,*
implied.
"Yes, sir. This is a pharmacy." I answer
softly, firmly, in my customary
pleasant manner.

He stomps off, cheated of the chance
to show his civic zeal. If only
I'd been fingering melons
at the greengrocers, he
could have hauled me off,
polished his pride
on my soft,
yet firm,
yellow star.

Night

Trapped in a cage. Iron walls,
my arms, beating—

Always, at night, an open window
ever a new night, over and over again.

Every landscape on this planet
in the always-different sky.

One has what wings one needs to fly across any walls
into a sky that knows of no...partitions.

Orchard Light

Stars catch in the bare trees
outside my window; glisten
like pears or apples picked
in some hungerless paradise.

They catch, then climb free,
or graze heaven's plain.

In a strange house, in a strange bed,
I take down the blackout paper, hear
two stars speaking:

'Wherever you are in the world
you will find us, always; know
yourself home.'

Music

We give the cold shoulder
to the Concertgebouw; prefer
our Schubert sung with a slap of Yiddish.

My brother plays with intensity, they say,
and his usual cool brilliance. Only I can see
how his hands pray to the piano.

And now my palm reader, with the dear,
dubious voice, goes on forever.
Patience!
Think of how, the last soirée

that lady of high nobility with the rich
profusion of blond curls on her forehead
sang like a Japanese
canary in labour.

Mystic

Cycling home from Courbetstraat, last night:
my arms my hair my thighs
streaming tenderness, everything
I could not give him.

At the little bridge over the canal,
I stood looking at the water, spring's
arms around me as I poured
all this love I could not show or speak
into starry water.

What is, what must be:
to vanish into the vastness of air, to break
the I through which this richness threads.
Not flight, but flowing.

What is there to understand?
The world, this world
happens to us, whether we
make sense of it or not. Blessed

abandonment: strict
surrender.

The Merchant from Enkhuizen

with his sack of kidney beans comes straight
from Dostoevski. He needs to learn the language
for commercial purposes. Not Chekhov's or Pushkin's Russian
but the words for seed catalogues, ledgers, price and volume.
For this, thank God: we can't eat *The Cherry Orchard*.

No Jews allowed in greengrocers' shops, or market stalls.
A fistful of beans for the price of a cow. Unless

you come across the merchant from Enkhuizen,
selling beans to us Yellowstars
for the price of beans, not diamonds.

He hands me a slice of cheese on bread
he has baked himself. Takes dictation,
reads aloud, as if we were just two
human beings together, each of us

made in God's image.

In the Bathroom

Never divide the great longing
into a host of small satisfactions.

Face slathered in cold cream,
feet firm on the coconut matting
(the two small dents
my knees have carved)
I know
I shall never marry.

Cranes and chrysanthemums
on my Japanese kimono,
its belt snug at my waist.

I don't think I have to put up
with one other person for life,
just with myself and with God.

Han

The flesh and only the flesh
...every lust summoned from its depths.

No longer my lover: a friend,
bed-partner, assuager
of appetite.

Let me warm you
with my body, let me pamper all
your small lusts.

For the times I lay naked
on the Persian rug beside the stove,
its flame our only light, and you
the man-at-hand: mere instrument.

For the times I sobbed into your armpit,
as you lay, happy and whole,
stretched out beside little

hypocrite me, pleasured
and desolate, still
wanting him so—

Scarcely younger than my father,
you and he.

My sentence:
to watch fiery and passionate lovers turn,
bit by bit, into old men.

Love

above the sheets, out-
side the skin:

this love I cannot own.
Always reaching.

Through the needle's eye
of an embrace it slips.

Open my hands: it flies.
All I hold is lack.

No means to say or show this love.
The vault of my heart: locked fingers.

Fallow

Rooted in this life
as in this earth, this
difficult soil, blood-watered,
paved with bootleather.

Immaterial anchorage
needful as air: my soul
splits the clay I root in;

floods field, steppe. Yet all
through the rich, the heavy dark
roots' thin, white needlework.

Filaments eclipse themselves:
no conditions,
no desires—

fallow.

Beethovenstraat

Man on a bicycle in Beethovenstraat—
what history book will spare you a footnote?
How your star sings gold on your chest
(saffron, colour of radiance).

History and poetry
have little to say to one another,
and it's true, my enchantment
glosses over so much. My brother,
for instance, his dirty raincoat, his star
frayed, flapping like a sick crow.

You wear yours like a sun in
that sky they can't steal. Our souls
as free as our bodies are barred.

To refuse
to weep, shriek, firework rage;
to believe in God, to believe in man,
to believe in self

without apology or argument.

Bombs and Bach

In another room, *The Goldberg Variations,* while
someone in yet another room
(next door, from the sound of it)
shoots at bombers overhead.

pianissimo-ack-ack

In all the anywheres
of Europe, houses crumpling like accordions,
demented percussion.

I lie back, listening to Bach take on
the bombers.
Needle skips, stutters, yet,
Bach, meaning *stream.*

No miracle of nature: just
one of us, as *Bruder Hitler*
is one of us. How can we fear
what we ourselves have made, or made up?
Something close to us
as the breath ruffling our lungs:

a stream, a scream.
No monsters. No miracles.
Just us.

The Bread Bin

I pursue my appetites to their most secret
and hidden lairs, and try to root them out.

Bernard sneaks an extra sandwich.
I turn on him as if he'd robbed the bank.
Bernard, half-starving, still-growing.

What I'd give for a good slice of bread thick with butter,
sprinkled with chocolate. Especially
bad at night, these cravings
for Bernard's sandwich.

I am not growing,
nor am I starved. And I know
I'll feel the worse for it in the morning.

Heel broken from a grey loaf.
Cucumber shaving, a
smear of tomato.

On imagination's tray
a cup of cocoa:
dreams dark as coffee beans.

Contentment

Longing is always greater than satisfaction...
But there are moments when there is neither
satisfaction nor longing.

Cross-legged, by the stove, I read Rilke.
Han smokes his pipe
over the evening paper.

'Hello, my dear old friend.'
'Hello, old girl.'

These long, lovely silences
in all this clanging,
as if our hearts had kissed.

Roof over our heads,
food in our bellies,
stove licking our skins.

Lament

And if you have given sorrow the space
its gentle origins demand,
then you may truly say: life
is beautiful, and rich.

I would be earth, but am only sand
the wind scatters.

Let the airplane over my head
drop its bomb, douse my life.
How much easier not to go on.

Cycling with this stone
in my basket, this foundling
swaddled in misery:

unwrap it, put it to your breast,
make sorrow the way you once
made love.

Soul

that discredited word, meaning
all that's disinterested,
dead to the urge to possess.

A soul is forged from fire,
rock crystal, is

tender as an eyelash.
a small closed-in centre
to which I describe the world outside
as I would to a blind man.

A vast, empty plain,
a vast, ripening cornfield
holding something
of God and Love.

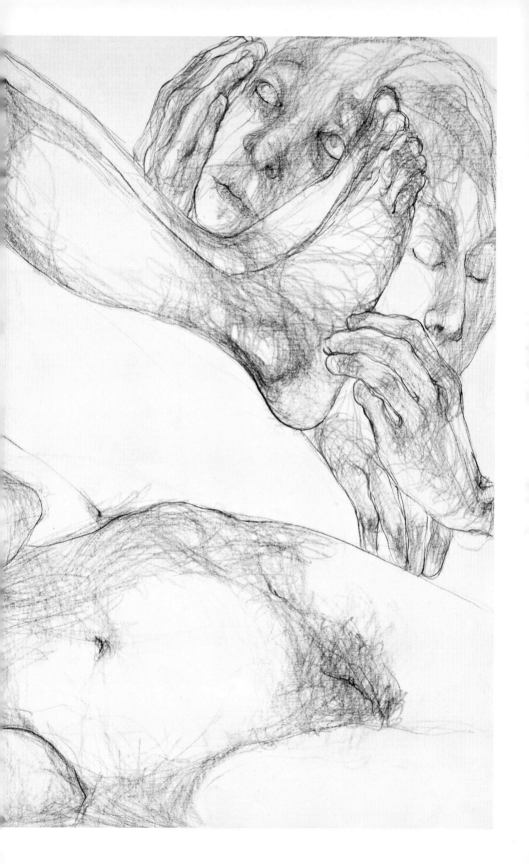

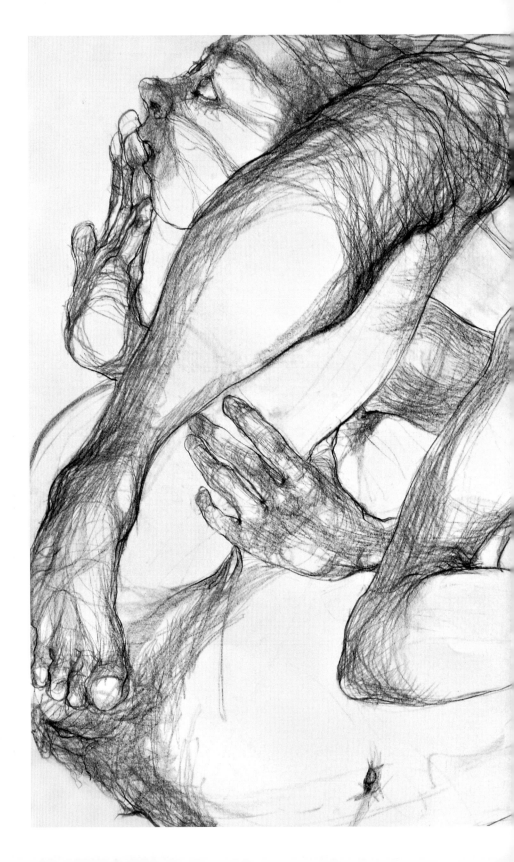

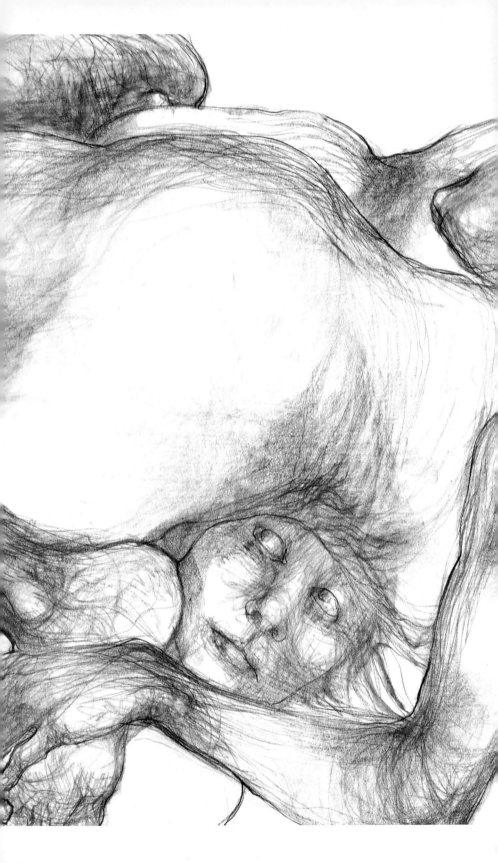

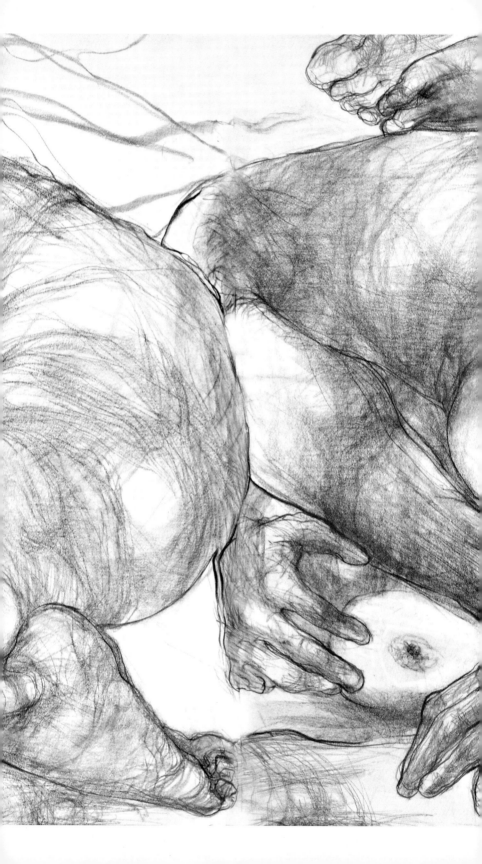

Skating Club, South Amsterdam

Along the quay, a breeze
like a warm mist,
a long drink of water.

Lilacs purse their purple horns,
more fruit than flower.
On the rosebushes
buds like baby teeth.

Sun combing my hair,
German soldiers, drilling.

Bicycle Thieves

Yellowstars are now forbidden bicycles
as well as trams.

Bicycle that was all my zest,
my north and south, my east, my west...

Braving all winds, wild horse
only I could tame.

I consign you to rust
and quiet, in a sadness worse
than any *animal post coitum.*

Taking what comes to me.
No picking, no choosing.

Suffering

Patience and suffering
mean the same thing, or else
patience is what confers
dignity upon suffering.

To bear this great weight
without burdening others.
To grow stronger through the bearing,
carrying my blood in drops of lead.

Strength that will never desert you, though
you would die, in three days, in a labour camp.

It is possible to create...by simply "molding"
one's inner life. And that, too, is a deed.

Wisdom

I who have decided to love mankind
instead of men,

to love life's contradictions,
impossibilities.

I who have grown into a fine old
philosopher, when suddenly

the telephone rings, his voice
prickling the length of my neck.

Or he teases me, calls me
sweet little goose
and my heart careens.

What we love in another
is the life in that person;
that is why we must never
seek to possess him.

sweet little goose

At the Dentist's

A touch of the bordello, these purple,
velvet chairs. Here, *The Book of Hours*
keeps me perfect company.

The dentist's drill a perverse indulgence.
Plugging holes
with silver & mercury bullets.

No lament, no complaint
for the time spent here, or at
the hairdresser's, or clearing up
after breakfast.

To be inside each moment,
however unmomentous: to be alive.

Despair I

No rejoicing in You today.
No great noise. My happiness
drags round in stone shoes
and a coat of bruised metal.

Even the trees outside my window.
Nothing but deadwood, now:
splinters in sky's eye.

Inside me, a lump,
Heavy, stagnant.

Ashes cake my heart. My face
a salted fish. Each bone a sieve
catching every grief.

Desiderata

Inner clarity, inner certainty,
harmony of spirit.

Patience and steadfastness.
Loyalty to myself: the courage
to brave the contempt of others,
their ridicule at how seriously
I take myself.

Insignificance. Humility.
Consistency between actions and ideals.
Solitariness (needing
neither mate nor lover).
Detachment. Freedom.

To make the difficult thing easy
without it becoming an untruth.
To find things out for myself—no
royal road, no knowledge
leading to power.

To accept myself as I am,
my right to be, as I am.
To chronicle the now.
To live to see the future.

Desk vs Double Bed

Since to breathe is to choose;
since crisis is our very air,
I make my choice.

The writing of a small piece of prose,
or a conversation about fundamental
life-and-death matters, a fellow human being
will always give me greater
and more lasting satisfaction than a marriage bed.

Sweet, salty marriage bed:
mere floating dock,
no port or harbour.

My only haven: a wooden plank
snowed with papers. A hyacinth
in a chocolate-sprinkles tin.
Pen, ink, notebook
ruled with lines blue as the eyes
of a northern sea.

Infinite waves, perpetual storms
and a paper boat, words
its only ballast.

Despair II

What is at stake is our impending destruction
and annihilation, we can have no more illusions...

How can I admit this into my heart,
that deep well of God in me?
They are out to destroy us completely.

Not just wear us down, sicken us
by arresting those who risk their lives,
bringing us bread bought
with ever-scarcer coins;

not just break us, like so many
tired bones, but shame us, too.
One section of the Jewish population...
helping to transport the majority
out of the country.

They mean to tamp, then scatter us:
earth to ash. Nobody's dust.

Eros

to drink from the cup of your mouth

Breathing together, heating
myself through, a long
bright burning.

One breath through the two of us.
Apart, I long for you, my skin
torn in two,

long to lie with you when
my body is dressed
in my soul.

You give me all your heart knows
and I want more, want
your whole body in mine.

Dictating a business letter, a report,
your hands caress my breasts and thighs,
even my eyelashes.

Or wrestling, mouths fused, bodies meshed.
Your *small messenger,* not to be budged, till
I take him in hand—and yet,

and yet.
I would sooner sleep
with books than with men.

Ethics

We cannot be lax enough in what we demand
of others and strict enough in what we demand of ourselves.

Always the fascination with burst metal,
burnt bodies. Creatures of adaptation that we are,
even to our own extinction.

If we cannot cry out, if we tame our fury and disgust,
we must gather round a pit of burning skin,
warming ourselves with all we can get used to.

Cry out your horror, but silence hate:
it will choke you to ashes without
the splendour of burning. To call for the death

of all 80 million Germans
because they have the power
to exterminate us—

save your strength for better things.

Family

I want no husband, no children no responsibility
for anyone but myself—and God knows that requires all my strength.

Mother, *mamushka*, refugee
from Russian pogroms, I have watched you
wolfing down soup in your blue lace dress.

Model of all I fear and refuse
to become: moaning, complaining, dressed to the nines,
whose love gushes out in chicken legs and boiled eggs.

I grew up in your madhouse, I
and my two mad brothers—the medical student,
the concert pianist. Eating your chicken soup,
reading Plato with Father.

He vists me now, while he still may,
small man in a checked scarf and crumpled
hat, bearing one,
just one
egg, and a pat of butter.

Father, the delivery man: *ton agathon*
and *oy nebbich.*
Even in the stench of a labour camp
he'd be happy reading Horace.

Mother, Father—let me keep you
as deep in me as I once lay in you.
Let me forgive you the bond
of having brought me here.

Despair III

There isn't a single kind thought in me,
I'm miserable and I hate everybody.

That fortress I build,
stone by slow stone,
with all the faith and courage I own—

Fifteen minutes' grief
can knock it down,
crush its foundations, drag
me under, yet

somehow I wash up
on another shore,
collecting pebbles,
scouting building stones.

Julius

All the logic and power of storms.
I might as well be walking blindfold
in a strange museum. All the breakage!

I can read Rilke on patience
till the cows learn to milk themselves.
Why can't I live the word
for more than an hour?

I want you for my own: now,
here. No pale
fiancée abroad, no harem hangers-on.
I want to own you, all of you

from balding head to false teeth, from
demon-swollen lower lip
to the flag folded beneath
your trouser buttons. And,

for all I cannot have, I want
others to suffer me.

Flowers

I bring them to my desk
as if to an altar: tulip bulbs,
red & white,
freesias, 3 pine cones
from Blaricum heath.

The opening
of a tea rose: proof enough
of the existence of God. Or
drinking the red-not-red
of sweetpeas, lovers' mad-reckless-red.

Cool, starry narcissi; chaste
green and white of snowdrops.
Cornflowers'
blue noon.

In a brown, earthenware pot,
on a small, white table
a forest of twigs, thick and dark enough
to get lost in.

The joy this pain brings,
this beauty.

That Kosher German Soldier

carrying his string bag of carrots &
cauliflowers, instead of a gun; his face
carved with a mouth instead of a screech-hole.

He pushes a note into Liesl's hand: she
reminds him so much of a rabbi's daughter
he had nursed on her deathbed, whole
days and nights.

I shall have to pray for him, too,
as well as for the rabbi.
A uniform plus a face, a voice
equals a soul, and all souls suffer.

No borders between souls.
No mere passport, prayer.

Quarry

No beautiful
schoolgirl's soul. No leaf or petal,
but granite, carved by currents. A workshop
never shut, without tools or engines,
powered only by something

trying to tear free in me,
to praise Your world,
this time, this place:
these blind and giant blocks.

God

I shall never be able to give thanks for my daily bread
when I know that so many others do not have theirs.
But I hope I shall be thankful even if I have, one day,
to go without that daily bread.

A deep well inside me,
choked with grit and stones. How often
must I take my bare hands
to dig You out?

You are not accountable to us.
If You were, how could You
be You? Yet we remain accountable—
how else can we stay human?

When You withdraw from me
every light in my body drowns.
Dawn blacks out the windows.

Listen: I do not
hold You responsible for all this—*if You*
cannot help me to go on
then I shall have to help You.

Packing for Transit

My hair,
thick and waving,
has been cut sensibly short.

Lipstick, rouge, perfume
all thrown away. Pretty blouses:
anything
sheer or silk. Even
aspirin.

In my rucksack, woollen vests, long
underwear, toothbrush,
sponge, an extra pair
of stout shoes.

Joy and faith.
Rilke, St Augustine,
an exercise book. And when
I can no longer write,
I'll have this one thing left:

to simply lie down and try
to be a prayer.

En route

My hub,
my home:
my desk.

On it
a tea rose,
a typewriter,
a reel of black cotton
a handkerchief—

Leave it.
Leave it all.
Leave it at this.

TWO

Westerbork

For us...it's no longer a question of living,
but of how one is equipped for one's extinction.

Drenthe Heath

is in and of the world, thus
there are flowers here,
yellow gorse and dark blue lupins
overspent, megalithic tombs.

Between barren heath and empty sky
the reeking, wooden barracks:
a village no Potemkin could disguise:
lice and fleas and all their hosts.

500 x 600 meters of mud, indigenous.
It breaks our shoes, eats at our feet.
Sand blown from blameless Saharas
scours our eyes.

Though many die here, it is the living dead
who beseech us, preparing for Transport:
thousands upon thousands of men, women, children
infants, invalids, the feeble-minded,
the sick and the aged who pass through our hands.

Steel-on-flint shouting of guards,
typewriters battering names, numbers:
the machine-gun fire of bureaucracy.

Artists and intellectuals, men
with professions, prowl the barbed wire,

gutted of all they had or were,
knifed by their shadows.

Emptiness framed
by earth, by sky,
filled only

by what we keep,
inside.

Credo

Whoever enters my innermost heart
I cannot abandon.

Whomever I love in my innermost heart
I must leave free.

I don't fool myself about the real
state of affairs, and I've even dropped the pretense
that I'm out to help others. I shall merely try

to help God as best I can, and if
I succeed in doing that, then I shall be
of some use to others.

Transport en famille

I can bear my burden, but not yours.
Mother, father, brother:
if we must travel together,
how can I watch you suffer?

Too much compassion
can be greed. Strive
for the detachment
the dressing shows to the wound.

The Thinking Heart of the Barracks

No books or pictures, here. No bright
shawls, or market flowers. Only

a small patch of sky,
and space enough to fold my hands.

All round me, women, girls,
snoring, sobbing, dreaming out loud.

And the ones who try to keep sane
by starving themselves of thought or feeling—

Though I am nothing but holes in a scraped-out shoe,
though the debris of a whole city drags my head down,

let me catch them, hold them,
think and feel enough for us all.

Stop me from playing, let me work, at last.
Keep me green and fallow.

Each day's horde of being:
nourished, listened to, known.

The Wild West Cabin

of the hospital canteen,
sawn from logs and stumps. Small windows rattle:
through them we see sandbanks, rough grass,
an empty railway truck.

Beyond the barbed wire, green billows
that could be spruce,
young spruce.

Sometimes we pretend we've found our way
to a mining camp in a Klondike

where nothing grows, and the only gold
grows on shallow-rooted teeth

or chill-blained, expendable fingers.

the pitifully thin, incessant wailing of the babies

To be massed, herded—this, already
is extinction. How, in this press,
can heart think, mind feel?

Easy to write in a sun lounge
or at my desk, in the shade of roses.
Needful to write here, now
where raw winds drill the barracks.

So many broken windows, yet the air still stinks.
We fight it down, as we do the sour
and watery soup.

Fleas, split socks, gouged heels
and faces. Sentient human beings,
picking over peas till their souls are small
as the grit in their eyes.

Children without parents
—the lost of the lost—
but worse, the babies dragged from their cots
in a merciless dark. Screams sharp
enough to thread needles.

Jews dragging off Jews. *Jewish big shots*
harvesting the sick and senile:

nothing is spared us,
even the worst
of our own.

Gulls

For a quarter of an hour
stolen from transport lists, ferocious stamps,
the sick and the sick with terror,
Joop and I watch gulls fly over Drenthe heath.

The laws that move them through these huge,
clouded skies were not made in Nüremberg;
have lasted longer than a thousand years.

Clouds darker than the purple lupins,
the impartial, punishing rain.
Black and silver birds
no more captive or free

than our hearts
pumping their stubborn, muscled wings.

THREE

Poland

*A sort of collective term for all
that is unknown about the future.*

Am Ende

The east to which you were so sure
you would travel, Etty: Russia's steppes, Japan:
that east ends here.

Hard *to roll melodiously from God's hand*, now.
To find life meaningful, beautiful, to call God good.
To be master of your inner resources.

This too is life, this *Tod-fabrik*.
If life is struggle, is suffering,
this place roars with life.

All those made in God's image, from babies
to *Musselmänner*. Could God
be a *Musselmann*, a dead-alive too weak to hold,
defend a dish and spoon?

This suffering, inflicted, not chosen,
by a maniac with a toothbrush moustache
and an undescended testicle.

No hunger, no cold, no filth;
no stench, no pain,
no knowing the pain of others
could make you hate.

Did you keep your promises?
To bear every moment.
even the most unimaginable, as it comes.

To pick You up if ever You should
stumble over me.

How I die will show me who I really am

In God's arms, or in His clutches?
Has He room for you and all those others
whose fate you fought to share?

Did you go into hiding,
at the very last, from Him?

There is room for everything in a single life.
For belief in God and a miserable end.

Coda

We left the camp singing—

A message brief enough for a postcard
thrown from a cattle car,
picked up, posted by some
anonymous Samaritan, or just a citizen

punctilious about litter and letters.

What matters now is this rescue
of a scrap of paper written by a woman,

aged 29, ex-secretary to a chirologist,
ex-teacher of Russian, student of God
and man.

A scrap of paper, letters, and seven notebooks
bear witness beyond
a mass grave. Words preserved
like fruit in glass jars. A quicksand
of questions:

If one only becomes creative,
even in one's saddest and most desperate moments,
then surely nothing else matters?
And a creative moment is surely not paid for
too dearly with suffering?

Etty Hillesum (1914-43) lived the last few years of her short life in Amsterdam, where she shared a house with friends, including a much older man, Han Wegerif, who became her lover for a time. She began her journals at the behest of Julius Spier, a Jewish refugee from Nazi Germany who had studied with Carl Jung, and who practised psychotherapy in the unusual form of chirology, or the reading of palms. Her relationship with Spier was intense, both spiritually and erotically.

Etty Hillesum refused to go into hiding, and volunteered to work at the Westerbork transit camp, from which the Jews of the Nether-lands, and other European countries, were shipped to death camps in the east. Etty Hillesum perished in Auschwitz, aged 29; her parents and both her brothers were also victims of the Shoah.

Many thanks to Novalis Press for their kind permission to quote excerpts from *Etty. The Letters and Diaries of Etty Hillesum 1941-1943*, by Etty Hillesum © NOVALIS Saint Paul University, Ottawa, Canada. Reproduced with permission of the publisher. www.novalis.ca.

Etty Hillesum

Monoprints and Conté Drawings ~ *Claire Weissman Wilks*

• in order of appearance •

Jasmine, monoprint on paper (detail), 2006, 61cm x 46cm

A Small Silent Voice, conté on paper, 1984, 99.5cm x 66cm

They Open Up Before Me, conté on paper, 1984, 70cm x 99cm

Ich Kannes Nicht Verstchen, Dass Die Rosen Blumen, or
I Know Not Why the Roses Bloom, conté on paper, 1984, 99.5cm x 66cm

There's Always Been a Splendid View from Here, conté on paper,
1984, 66cm x 99.5cm

Transport Boulevard, conté on paper, 1984, 99.5cm x 66cm

The Wailing of the Babies Grows Louder Still...
It Is Almost Too Much to Bear, a Name Occurs to Me, Herod,
conté on paper, 1984, 99.5cm x 66cm

I Have Broken My Body Like Bread and Shared It Out
Among Men (seven page spread fold out), conté on paper/triptych,
1984, 300cm x 66cm

Untitled, monoprint on paper (detail), 2006, 81cm x 61cm

Untitled, monoprint on paper (detail), 2006, 81cm x 61cm

Untitled, monoprint on paper (detail), 2006, 81cm x 61cm

III

The Waste Zone

with photographs
by
Goran Petkovski

With my own eyes I saw, Sedna, wife of the seabird,
moaning and lamenting and asked her,
'Why do you weep, proud Sedna?'
And she answered, 'Cold winds blow about my bed;
there are no lamps. I am hungry and wretched.
Aya, my father, come and take me home.'

I The Burial of the Commons

　　April is the cruellest month, breeding
protest in the lulled land, mixing
tear gas and champagne, bruising
true, patriot roots with chain link, concrete.
Winter worried us, melting ice caps,
thawing perma frost, thwarting
migration patterns of the caribou.
Summer threatens the usual astonishments:
floods and tornados, forest fires, drought. Acts
10　of God's self-appointed annointed. Near Ajax
on exhaust-clogged 401, we pass Travelodge,
its giant TM Teddy Bear (blue jacket, socks
and stocking cap) packaging instant
innocence. My husband drives; the kids
sleep. I read, much of the way, *Little Dorrit,*
as the car crawls east.

　　What are the roots that clutch, what branches grow
out of asphalt, out of grass
parched beneath
20　styrofoam cups and plastic bags? Citizen,
how can you speak out, knowing from web and net,
newspaper columns, television screens
the global picture. From hardwoods' ashy foam, the dying
arms of winter, from a few pared bones
of birch, hidden miracles of sap and leaf.
Somewhere north are rivers
of jade silk, and mountain crocus
springs from lichen-scribbled rock. When we came back,
late, from Miles Canyon, our faces wet with spray,

eyes peeled of billboards, logos, we were
alive, open
as our freely empty hands:
  épilation au Laser Diode
  varices, rides, collagène
Truckers lunge past, underpaid and underslept.
The Last Battle—kids wake
to read aloud how Shift talks poor, dim
donkey Puzzle into wearing godly
Lion's skin. Clennam draws from Pancks
"The Whole Duty of Man in a commercial country":
business, i.e. squeeze the poor to oil the rich.
50% exchange rate on US currency
at gas stations near Kingston. *Win Points:*
Redeem Your Points. Nearly nine, blue
thickens into black, the kids now singing
un Canadien errant
bani de ses foyers.

 Madame Shelagh, famous *clairparlante*
has a bad cold, nevertheless
is known to be the wisest woman in Canada
with a wicked laugh. Here,
says she, are twin sister-students, and the Lady of Protests.
(Once, those rubies were your eyes. Look!)
Here is Lady Liberty, on stilts
the lady of crisis situations.
Here is the globe and here the Star-Striped
Phallus, fucking it up.
And here the water-cannon; here are
one-eyed, double-dealing merchants, and this page,

60 which is blank, is something they carry in attaché cases
which you are forbidden to see. I do not find
The Statesman. Fear death by choking.
I see crowds of people, watching, and stricken,
falling back and pushing forward.

  Unreal City,
Under the blue & white of *fleurs-de-lys*
a crowd flowed into *Place du Théatre*, so many
I had not thought dissent could rouse so many.
Cheering and explosions,
70 bandannas dipped in lemon vinegar, plywood-
blinded windows. Riot cops studded in rows, blocking
side streets. There I saw one I knew
and stopped him, crying: 'Stevens!
'You who were on NAFTA's side!
'That corpse you planted in this country's garden—
'has it sprouted into this? Or has civil discontent
'disturbed its bed? Oh keep Watch Dog far hence, that's friend to men
'or with his nails he'll dig it up again!
'You! Hypocrite free-trader—*mon semblable*,
80 '*mon frère!*'

II *'Partie d'échecs' dans Saint-Jean-Baptiste*

The Chair he sat in, like a brandished throne,
Glowed on the marble, where the glass
Held up by secret servicemen
From which a high-tech monitor peeped out
(Another hid his gun beneath the vest
Of an Armani suit) doubled the boyish head
While on the roof of Loew's Concorde Hotel
Heat-seeking missiles did sleep fitfully, awaiting
Signs of fury 'mongst the populace
90   Shut out by a million-dollar fence
3 metres high and 4k long.
Above the shamrocked mantel was displayed
As though a window gave upon the urban scene
The Rape of We the People, by the barbarous
King, so rudely forcing outer space
To weave a somewhat violable shield.
And still the special envoys press, and still the world recoils
The force be with you trapped in dirty ears.
And other presidents and withered stumps of rule
100   Waited on his pleasure; jaded reporters
Leaned out from microphones, while aides
Hummed 'Pomp and Circumstance,'
Faraway clashes all shut out.
Under the teleprompter (media room
Provided by CISCO systems) his tongue
Lunged into words, then would be vacantly still.

'What am I thinking? What thinking. What?
I never know what I am thinking. Think.'
    'I think this planet's up shit creek

137

without a paddle.'
'What is that noise?'
    Tear gas exploding.
'What is that noise now? What are the protestors doing?'
    Nothing again nothing.
                                'Do
'You know nothing? Do you see nothing? Do you remember
'Nothing?'

 I remember
Liberty, Democracy, Prosperity. Savings and Loan.
'Did they catch you out, or not? Is there nothing in your head?'
                                        But

O O O O that Noam Chomskyan Rag
It's irreverent,
so intelligent.
'What shall I do now? What shall I do?'
'I cannot rush out as I am, and walk the street
'Without my spin doctors, my make-up men.
'What shall we do tomorrow?
'What shall we ever do?'
Opening Ceremonies at six
Or, if delayed for security reasons,
A speech on H-I-V-A-I-D-S.
First Wives will promenade, and then the Family Foto Op
Against the Plains of Abraham.

 When Lil's doctor cut out the lump, I said—
I didn't mince words, I said
Now you've had your warning, smarten up.
Get off the cancer sticks, like the doctor told you.
He did, I was there, he said

140   'It's in your hands—not just your lungs—
whether you pull out of this.'
Fruit Smoothie and a Veggie Maxie Melt!
You've been killing yourself for years, I said
and if you don't stop like that (I snapped
my fingers) they'll shut you in a box
before you've had to start to dye your hair.
You ought to be ashamed, you
with young kids and all. 'I can't
help it,' she said, pulling a long face.
150   'When I cut the fags I eat enough
for six: french fries and pizza and Big Macs.'
You *are* a fool, I said.
Don't you ever watch tv? Even Oprah's
off ground beef. *Fruit Smoothie
and a Veggie Maxie Melt!*
Come round to me for sprouts
and tofu—that time you came to stay
when Bill went on a binge
I served a pot of curried-carrot soup
160   and you just snorted up the steam
to get the beauty of the spice. *Last call
for lunch, Last call, last call
Fruit Smoothie and a Veggie Melt!*

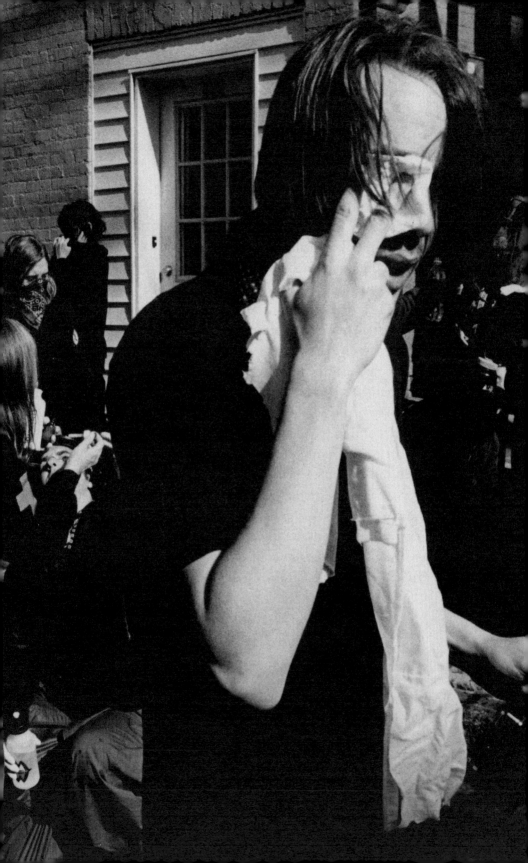

III Tear Gas Sermon

The river's seal is broken: final shards of ice
crammed along the banks. Wind
barely skims the water. The Iroquois are
   departed.
Mighty Saint Laurent/Saint Lawrence
shrugging its weight of garbage bags, sour bottles,
170   condoms, mateless shoes, newspapers, fast-food cartons
or other testament of human life. The Iroquois
are departed for reserves with poisoned wells,
and their persecutors,
the loitering heirs of civil servants, departed
along with our MPs. In the green zone, beneath the overpass
we rest, squeezing chemicals from lidless eyes...
assis au bord d'un fleuve
au pays étranger
But at our backs in rancid gusts we hear
180   volleys of tear gas, and water cannons pulling near.
A boy crept slowly from the street
bearing a box of donuts to the fence;
amid the laughter of the jeaned, tee-shirted crowd
he offered tim bits to the plexi-glassed and armoured cops.
They fired tear gas, then, when he'd returned
to join his friends, lashed out with rubber bullets.
Farther along, Black Blocks were launching smoke bombs,
ball bearings, hockey pucks. Rave rhythms beaten out
on lampposts, guard rails, while overhead we hear
190   the throb of helicopters, which shall bring
Dubya to Johhny Christian in the spring.
O the sun shines bright on Mr Bush
and his bush-leaguers:

they brush their teeth in bottled water.
Et, O ces cris de manifestants près de la clotûre!

   Recule—get back,
put on your masks—*We're*
Canadians, dammit!
So rudely forc'd.

200   Unreal City
Under the white fog of six thousand cannisters,
having paid a cool $500,000, I then asked
Mr Piranha, a Colombian merchant,
clean-shaven, with a pocket full of coke
(top-grade product, ingredients on demand)
to lunch at the Convention Centre
followed by a weekend at the Château Frontenac.

   At the blue-black hour, when throngs
of protestors thin out,
210   I, Trudeau, though dead, unable
not to see or hear, at the twilit hour, when blue
thickens into black, regard the pensioner, whose window
overlooks the fence, whose throat's stung raw, whose eyes tear
uncontrollably. Madeleine Parent, a union activist
for sixty years, and nameless others
weaving balloons and paper flowers
through the mesh; leaving crayoned signs:
Compassion, Cité a Vendre! The wall of shame, breached first
on Friday, corner of René Lévesque and rue
220   de l'Amérique Française. Kids with carabiniers,
straight from Outward Bound. And then
gassing of first aid station, the Zone Vert

(safe to bring children to). No state of apprehended
insurrection (I, Trudeau, have suffered
and foresuffered all) enacted in a different city,
I, who in my time, called out the troops,
then walked the streets, with neither fear nor pity.
60,000 marching from Vieux Port,
dressed-up as butterflies, as Fidel look-alikes
230   all heading peacefully along rue de la Pointe des Lièvres
while in the *quartier* of St-Jean-Baptiste,'
Our Lady Liberty, hosed from her stilts
brought weeping to brute concrete, down.
With hooded eyes I watch negotiators, bureaucrats
(the time is now propitious, as they guess
the watchers sleepy, sated)
lay down laws to small, impoverished states:
Chapter 11, trade remedies,
TRIPS. Flushed and decided, they assault at once;
240   encounter no defence: Honest-to-God Free Traders
make a welcome of sheer impotence,
bestow one final, patronising kiss
One Big Family of the Americas
and grope their way, finding
security in conference rooms remiss...

   Mounties seal off the vents
where smoke bombs, tear gas filter in;
tight throats, red eyes in limousines
transporting dignitaries to their dinners,
250   while protest medics, scarlet crosses on their backs
treat activists and witnesses.
Si tu vois mon pays, mon pays malheureux.
Mon pays ce n'est pas un pays, c'est l'Etat.

'This music crept by me upon the waters'
and along Boulevard Charest Est.
O city, city, I can sometimes hear
the chanting of marchers from Laval,
or at parc Amérique-Française, where
squads of riot cops march single-file,
260   to serenades from five lone protesters:
'That's the Sound of Men,
Working on the Chain, Chai-ai-ain.'

        The river sweats
        Oil and tar
        The barges drift
        with the turning tide
            Qui va là?
            soldats du roi
        Wolfe and Montcalm
270   Reagan-Mulroney
this is what democracy looks like:
400 rubber bullets, 392
arrests

    Snow piled against crocus grenades.
'Moose Jaw bore me. A Quebec City prison
holds me, without water
or blankets or a word with a lawyer.'

    Traitors, not
traders. Some are Guilty.
280   *All are Responsible.*

144

My feet are at the fence, a rubber bullet
in my throat. After the attack
no one apologized, promising
'a new start.' I could make no statement.
What, they asked, could I resent?

The people, united
can never be defeated. My people
immigrants who expect
nothing from this place
but peace and quiet.

To *Vieux Québec* we came
Tear gas burning burning burning
O Maude, thou pluckest me out
O Maude thou pluckest

burning

IV   Violence by Teddy Bears

Jaggi the activist, three weeks in jail
for lobbing soft toys at police
(possession of dangerous weapons, they said).
Columnists tried him
300   in newsprint courts. As he rose or fell,
lawyers for the Constitution found his basic rights
had all been violated.
Right or Left
O you who pay taxes, vote, and watch the evening news,
consider Jaggi, captive and free as you.

V What the Prime Minister Said

   After the choking and vomiting
after the frosty silence in the convention centre
after the stone throwing and arrests
cellphones blaring, water-butt drumming
prison and château and reverberation
—sound bites and photo ops—
democracy enclaused.
We who once were citizens are now consumers
and consumed.

   Here is no water but only sickness, death:
e coli, cryptosporidium
poisoned aquifers from factory farms, liquid manure
soaking the earth like putrid syrup.
If there were water, we could bathe and drink.

   Who is the one walking beside you, wearing balaclava
and gas mask?
Or the one gliding across digital screens,
wrapt in a soft grey suit, white cashmere shirt?
What has he offered you to cross the vast, cold sea,
his song enchanting, his promises golden
     You will never know hunger
I will bring you all your heart desires.

   What is that sound high in the air
murmur of human lamentation
death squads, child prostitutes, *disparecidos*?
What is the city over the mountains
cracks and reforms and fibre optics in the blue-black air?

Glassed-in towers
Seattle, Prague, Washington, Davos
Unreal

    A woman drew her long black hair out tight
in knots her finger stumps could not untie.
Shamans with moon-pure faces fell
through icy mists of dreams; they sang to her,
340   and combed her hair. She told them
where to hunt the seal; where whales
blow fountains on the leaden sea.

    In this decayed hole among the tar sands
in sunlight and moonlight, the wind sighs blind
through stands of seedless soybean, corn.
Round-Up Ready birth defects; harvesting
only the finest genes. GM foods can harm no one.
Tobacco, they said, could harm no one.
Impose, the specialists decree,
350   market forces upon poverty.

    The pain and suffering of Mexico's poor
has grown worse as the result of the 'monstrous fraud'
of free trade, a delegation of Canadian church leaders has charged.
Vincente Fox says the FTAA will in time improve the lives
of the 40 million poor people in his country, 40%
of the population.
Hurry Up, Please, it's Time

    The snow had melted after the weekend's glare,
clouds dragged grey bellies, and nascent leaves

waited for rain
Ya basta!
Médecins sans Frontières: what have we given?
My friend, blood shaking our hearts,
stitching slashed flesh,
mass graves exhumed
to read the print of bones.
Ya basta!
Amnesty International: we have heard the key
turn in the door, once, almost forever.
370 We fight for keys,
all, in our prisons,
fighting for keys, each confirms the right
to jailbreak. Day and Night, rumours of
postcards, letters
(*I respectfully request you free this person*
guilty of nothing but humanity)
revive, sustain
a Nelson Mandela
Ya basta!
380 *World Literacy:* Their tongues responded
fluently to eyes expert with alphabet and ink.
The page was calm, their hearts
responded without shame or panic, reading
hope into each buoyant word.
High tech stocks are falling down falling down falling
down.
Tous pour le protocole de Kyoto—sauf un.
Blah blah blah. *Vive*
la Résistance!
390 *Cold winds blow about my bed*

there are no lamps.
These struggles we have launched
against our ruin. *Avance,*
    recule...défends...repose
et recommence.

Notes on *The Waste Zone*

The title of this poem is suggested both by T.S. Eliot's *The Wasteland*, and the Summit of the Americas held April 19-21, 2001 in Québec City to agree to the creation, by 2005, of a $17 trillion trade bloc: the Free Trade Area of the Americas or *Zone Libre Echange des Amériques*—encompassing 800 million people. The summit, it has been calculated, cost Canadian taxpayers at least $100 million (V. *The Toronto Star*, 23/04/01, A1.) The Interim Report by the Public Complaints Commission into events in Québec City has accused the RCMP of brutal police tactics involving the use of tear gas, stun grenades, rubber bullets and tazers, and of a serious abuse of power and authority in breach of the Charter of Rights and the Criminal Code. It is worth noting that the Commission has the right to air grievances but not to enforce change; it has no power to enforce its findings. Literally, the Waste Zone is the cityscape of Québec, poisoned by the clouds of chemicals used to separate witnesses and protestors from the 34 Heads of State, their aides, and members of the corporate elite participating in the summit; allegorically it is the entire global zone now open to unregulated commercial exploitation.

Inuit legend recounts how the beautiful maiden Sedna, seduced by a fulmer, or grey and white seabird, in the shape of a man, flees with him across the ocean. When her father, Aya, visits Sedna's new home he finds that instead of the ample food, warmth, and happiness the fulmer promised her, Sedna has been given only poverty and wretchedness. Aya murders the treacherous fulmer and flees with his daughter to the small boat in which they hope to return to their own land. The fulmer's kinsmen magically provoke a storm to avenge the murder; as the waves leap into his boat, Aya throws his daughter overboard. When Sedna clings to the side of the boat, Aya chops off the first digits of her fingers with his knife; when she makes one more desperate effort to hold on, he severs her fingers at the knuckle. Appeased, the fulmers disappear; Aya pulls his drowning daughter into the boat, and the two make land at last. Full of bitterness towards her father, Sedna orders her dogs to gnaw off the sleeping Aya's hands and feet; Aya curses her and the earth splits open, pulling father and daughter into Adlivun, a place beneath land and sea.

To a work of social, economic and cultural anthropology I am indebted in general, one which has already had a profound influence on our generation: I mean Naomi Klein's *No Logo*. Anyone who is acquainted with this critique of corporate globalization will immediately recognize in the poem certain references to modes and ceremonies of resistance.

I The Burial of the Commons

Line 7. One of George W. Bush's first acts as president was to cancel the agreement made between the Gwich'en people and former U.S. president Bill Clinton, to prevent exploitation of oil and gas reserves in the ancestral breeding and migration grounds of the caribou on which the traditional life of the Gwich'en people depends.

8. For a random sampling of such "astonishment" see "Diary of the Planet," by Steve Newman, *The Toronto Star*, 21/04/01 B5. Newman takes note of the following climatic events transpiring in the week before the summit: a transpacific dust cloud carrying pollution from Asia across the Pacific to the western U.S. and Canada; flooding of the Mississippi; an earthquake in China, along with perceptible earth movements in Japan, northern Pakistan, east Nepal, central Italy, northern Colombia, El Salvador and northeast British Columbia; thunder and hailstorms in Houston Texas causing $75 million in damages to homes and businesses; an eruption of Mexico's Mt. Popocatepetl; tropical cyclone Alistair over the Sarafura Sea between Australia and New Guinea, and in Orissa, India, a rampage of elephants driven by deforestation into populated areas.

29. Miles Canyon, near Whitehorse, Yukon, is a spot of great and unspoiled natural beauty. Among the rocks above the river blooms one of the earliest signs of spring: the Manitoba crocus, also known as the pasque flower.

33-4. Advertisement for space-age depilatory methods, appearing *in Le Journal de Québec* the weekend of the summit.

40. Dicken's fierce critique, in *Little Dorrit*, on unregulated stockmarket speculation and unrestricted material consumption by the wealthy, at the expense of society's poorest, is not irrelevant in this context.

48. Shelagh Rogers, host of CBC Radio's now-defunct *This Morning* interviewed three protestors from the Québec summit on Monday April 23, 2001. Two were twin sisters, university students, from Moose Jaw, Saskatchewan; the other was an experienced, older activist.

53. The effect of exposure to tear gas is not only severe irritation of the eyes, but also choking, vomiting and disorientation. "Over 80 countries have signed the Geneva Convention that bans the use of tear gas. There is little information about the long-term effects of the toxic gas used. There are concerns that it may cause cancer...." Handout: "What Really Happened in Québec City" PublicInquiry@ziplip.com

54-57. Lady Liberty and the Star-Striped Phallus were part of the protest march from Laval University on the afternoon of Friday, April 20, 2001.

73-74. V. Sinclair Stevens' article on the experience of being gassed at Québec City: "A Police State in the Making," published on April 24, 2001, in *The Globe and Mail*. Stevens was minister of regional expansion under Brian Mulroney, and an MP from 1972-1988.

II *Partie d'échecs' dans Saint-Jean-Baptiste*

The title for this section is a newspaper heading from *Le Journal de Québec*, 22/04/01, p. 5. It is preceded by the words. "Le Black Bloc Frappe Encore:" Le Black Bloc a encore frappé, hier, débarquant massivement dans le quartier St-Jean-Baptiste pour se frotter à des policiers à la mèche beaucoup plus courte que la veille. Telle une petite armée bien organisée, les extrémistes du Black Bloc ont multiplié les offensives, non pas aux dépens des commerçants qui avaient fermés leurs portes ou placardé leurs vitrines, mais contre les forces de l'ordre et 'le symbole' de la lutte antimondialistes dont la 'manif pépère' ne suffit pas: le 'Mur de Québec....'" Décidés à ne pas céder un pouce de terrain, les policiers les ont également acceuillis avec deux camions-incendies aux jets d'eau d'une pression de 250 livres. Ils ont aussi tiré des salves et des salves de gaz lacrymogènes et de balles de caoutchouc. *Escouade de choc* Généreusement 'gazés', les protestataires se sont repliés dans le quartier Saint-Jean-Baptiste pour poursuivre cette 'partie d'échecs' vers 14h 45. C'est alors que plusieurs dizaines 'd'hommes en noir'—rien à voir avec les services secrets américains—masqués ont fait leur entrée. Formés principalement d'Américains, le Black Bloc constitué pour le Sommet de Québec a attaqué le périmètre de sécurité ceinturant la rue Saint-Jean, aux abords du centre des congrès.... En soirée, il devenait périlleux de sortir de chez soi, dans ce quartier, à moins d'être muni d'un masque à gaz.

81. The conspicuously imperial style befitting the U.S. president was attested to by a Toronto journalist whose plane was delayed in taking off from Québec City: "On the tarmac, we wait for Air Force One to leave since, our captain explains, no one may take off beside or before the presidential jet—anywhere in the world. It makes me think of journalist Tom Walkom's explanation of the fence: it was really built to protect protestors from the US Secret Service. If any of them had got inside the perimeter, those agents would have come out of the Loew's hotel with guns blazing. Their idea of anybody else's sovereignty is something that inevitably interferes with their own."

102. Elgar's "Pomp and Circumstance" was played as the leaders of the 34 nations participating in the summit entered the room where the opening ceremonies took place.

107. Germane to President Bush's off-cited intellectual difficulties may be this observation from a summit reporter at *The Toronto Star* : "He left many confused by his

statements that environmental and labour standards need to be protected in the FTAA deal, but on the other hand those protections must contain nothing that would 'destroy the spirit of free trade.'" *The Toronto Star*, 23/04/01 A8.

118. The Savings and Loan Scandal, which erupted under the presidency of the current president's father, George Bush, has been declared by senior economist Felix Rohatyn to have had the most devastating impact on the pocket of the average American this century, after World War II.

120. Prominent scholar and public intellectual, Dr. Noam Chomsky did not participate in the protests at Québec, but is an outspoken opponent of corporate globalization as well as U.S. foreign policy in general. Well known works by Chomsky include *The Political Economy of Human Rights* (with Edward S. Herman) and most recently *Hegemony or Survival* and *Failed States: The American Empire Project*.

129. "U.S. President George W. Bush just can't seem to get it right," observed a summit journalist, "even when he tries. Speaking to the other leaders on Saturday, he

mentioned efforts to combat infectious diseases, such as 'H-I-V-A-I-D-S,' carefully enunciating each letter." *The Globe and Mail*, 23/04/02, A9. This rather uncharitable observation is of some interest, however, in view of the fact that on this very week-end of the Québec Summit, in an effort to stem the PR disaster caused by their

attempt to enforce First World prices in Third World economies, the world's richest drug makers withdrew from the legal battle to stop South Africa from importing generic AIDS drugs to help the 4.7 million South Africans stricken with the disease. More than 25 million Africans were living with AIDS in 2001.

III Tear Gas Sermon

171. V. a May 2001 email 'joke' that first appeared, apparently, on the pages of *The Ottawa Citizen*: "Can you imagine working for a company that has a little more than 300 employees and has the following statistics:

30 have been accused of spousal abuse

9 have been arrested for fraud

14 have been accused of writing bad checks

95 have directly or indirectly bankrupted at least 2 businesses

4 have done time for assault

55 cannot get a credit card due to bad credit

12 have been arrested on drug related charges

4 have been arrested for shoplifting

16 are currently defendants in lawsuits

62 have been arrested for drunk driving in the last year

It is the 301 MPs in the Canadian parliament, the same group that cranks out hundreds of new laws designed to keep the rest of us in line." What the email joke could have added was that these MPs had just voted themselves a 20% raise in salary.

177. The story of the tear-gassed donuts was recounted by Olivia Brown, a student and campus newspaper representative from the University of Guelph. Ms Brown was hit by a rubber bullet while in the act of peacefully observing the protest.

183. The activities of the Black Block activists were a source of much contention, both in the media and among the protestors at Québec.

195. "How does it feel to be raped? This is what happened to our city and to democracy." Claude Gaudreau, Québec City resident, quoted in *The Toronto Star*, 23/04/01, A6.

198. While ordinary people and well-informed specialists on public policy were forbidden, by the chain-link fence, from speaking to any of the 34 leaders or their bureaucrats, members of the business community who could pay $500,000 to sponsor a coffee break or other convivial events were permitted at such events to address and mingle with the summit guests.

206. Pierre Elliott Trudeau (1919-2000), imagined as a ghostly spectator and not, of course, as an actual participant at the summit of the Americas, is yet the most important personage in the poem, uniting all the rest. The public outpouring of grief at Trudeau's death and the collective, civic experience of remembering the Trudeau era not only united Canadians across the country, but also threw into sobering relief our perception of the widespread lack of vision, intelligence and integrity among many of our current politicians. Trudeau's legacy, of course, is contentious; he is notorious for his suspension of civil liberties during the Québec crisis of 1970 as well as celebrated for his support of civic rights and freedoms, notably his declaration that the state has no right in the bedrooms of the nation.

224. Regarding the peaceful march of the People's Summit, *Le Journal de Québec* observed: "l'impressionante foule était aussi hétéroclite que multiculturelle." 22/04/01, p. 6.

234. As observed in an article in *The Toronto Star* 23/04/01, A6, Prime Minister Jean Chrétien would seem to have a paradoxical take on "Chapter 11"—arguably the most threatening feature of globalized and corporate-driven free trade, and named for its place in the North American Free Trade Agreement Act: "Discussing free trade, Chrétien seemed largely unaware of his own government's concerns about the controversial investor protection mechanisms in NAFTA. The measures allow corporations to launch lawsuits directly against governments if the companies feel their rights have been violated. Governments are concerned about their ability to maintain their own standards on the environment and International Trade Minister Pierre Pettigrew has said Canada would not sign a hemispheric free trade pact containing similar provisions. But Chrétien said the investor protection measure has worked well in NAFTA." A few days earlier, the same newspaper offered the following information: "A number of challenges by corporations have convinced critics the

investor-state provisions in NAFTA undercut the rights of elected governments to set and enforce their own rules. In 1997, Virginia-based Ethyl Corp. was awarded $13 million in damages and Ottawa acted to remove a ban on a gasoline additive after the company challenged Canadian regulations that banned the additive for fear it posed an environmental and health hazard. In February, a NAFTA tribunal ruled Canada had violated its obligations to the American waste disposal company S.D. Myers. The company is claiming $20 million in damages for losses after Ottawa banned PCB waste exports." *The Toronto Star*, 20/04/01, A6. TRIPS, or trade-related intellectual property rights were at stake in South Africa's legal victory over pharmaceutical corporations. Regarding trade remedies, see *The Globe and Mail*, 23/04/01, A8: "For FTAA to work, the U.S. would have to restrain its use of the 'so-called' trade remedy laws which are used to counter what the Americans decide are unfair subsidies or the dumping of products. These trade remedy laws have been sacrosanct in Congress. Canada's attempt to negotiate some limitation of their application under the North American free-trade agreement failed utterly, as has any attempt under the World Trade Organization."

239. Novelist John le Carré provides an insightful view on the dynamics of family relations in the arena of *Weltpolitik*: "The Cold War provided the perfect excuse for Western governments to plunder and exploit the Third World in the name of freedom; to rig its elections, bribe its politicians, appoint its tyrants and, by every sophisticated means of persuasion and interference, stunt the emergence of young democracies in the name of democracy." Columnist Joey Slinger extends le Carré's analysis to the realm of The Global Market: "Now we're saddled with 'a ludicrous notion,' one as beloved by George W.'s conservatives as by Tony Blair's New Labour: 'It holds to its bosom the conviction that, whatever the vast commercial corporations do in the short term, they are ultimately motivated by ethical concerns, and their influence upon the world is therefore beneficial.'" John Le Carré, "In Place of Nations," *The Nation*, quoted by Joey Slinger, *The Toronto Star* 21/04/01, A2. V. also Shawn McCarthy's analysis in *The Globe and Mail*, 23/04/01, A8: "Mr Bush is looking to secure protection for U.S. corporations active in Latin America. A free-trade agreement would be a far neater approach than resorting to sponsoring military coups and undermining left-wing governments, an approach the Americans have used in the past when their economic interests were threatened."

264-5. Students of Canadian history will need no reminder that the destiny of what is now Canada was decided in a climactic battle on the Plains of Abraham between the French forces of the Marquis de Montcalm and the British troops of General

James Wolfe. Both leaders lost their lives in the confrontation, a fate which signally did not occur to Ronald Reagan and Brian Mulroney, the chief participants in the 1985 "Shamrock Summit" at Québec City, which paved the way for the implementation of NAFTA.

265. "Jamais, à Québec, sauf peut-être pendant la conquête de la nouvelle-France par l'Angleterre... n'aura-t-on connu un climat de tension et de violence comme celui d'hier." *le Journal de Québec*, 22/04/ 01, 3.

266. One of the slogans painted on banners hoisted during the summit. Other italicised statements are similar slogans, or chants heard during the weekend's marches.

273-6. V. line 48—this was the fate of one of the twin sisters from Moose Jaw, as heard on CBC's *This Morning*.

280. "Eric Laferrière was shot in the throat with a plastic bullet travelling at 1000 metres/sec from a distance of 10-20 metres." "What Really happened in Québec city" PublicInquiry@ziplip.com.

290. One striking aspect of the police response to witnesses, demonstrators and activists at the Québec Summit was the fact that both those peacefully observing the activities at the fence and those making concerted efforts to dismantle the fence, and hitting back at riot police with molotov cocktails and paving stones, were teargassed, hit with rubber bullets and, in some cases, arrested.

291. Maude Barlow of the Council of Canadians was an outspoken opponent of NAFTA, and proved instrumental in halting the Multilateral Agreement on Investment (MAI). *The Toronto Star* quoted Barlow's response to a partial draft of the proposed hemispheric free trade pact leaked on 18/04/01. "'What's being negotiated in Québec city is NAFTA-plus.... It confirms our worst fears and will only strengthen the backbone of our movement." *The Toronto Star* 19/04/01, A6.

IV Violence by Teddy Bears

294. Jaggi Singh, a former University of Toronto student, was arrested in 1997 at the Vancouver summit for Asia-Pacific Economic Co-operation, and charged with the offence of speaking too loudly into a bullhorn, a charge subsequently dropped. Associated with the *CLAC* or Anti-Capitalist Convergence, Singh was jumped by plainclothes police and bundled into an unmarked van on the afternoon of Friday, April, 19 2001. For a number of days nothing was heard of his whereabouts. V. *La Presse, Montréal, 22/04/01*, A3 and *Le Journal de Québec, 21/04/01*, 14.

295. Following news of Jaggi Singh's arrest, protests were organized to bring public scrutiny to bear on the motives for, as well as the methods of, this activist's terrorist-style arrest and prolonged detention. An email circulating post summit can be taken as typical of this wave of organizing, and the carnivalesque form it has assumed: "Members of Bearly Able to Breathe, an ad hoc group of Toronto deglobalization activists and stuffed animals, are demanding an immediate public inquiry into the police tactics used in Québec City. The group will be staging a "Teddy

Bear's Picnic" prior to a rally opposing the Business Council on National Issues, to be held Tuesday May 8 [The BCNI...is made up of the nation's 150 most powerful CEOs and is Canada's most powerful lobby group.]...Anna Dashtgard, speaking on behalf of the stuffed animals, stated that: 'Our objective is to make Canadians understand that the use of toxic chemicals against civilians is a threat to all of our democratic rights'.... The group also voices serious concerns for those remaining in jail in Québec city. 'The symbol of the teddy bear is completely appropriate. Jaggi Singh had been wrongfully imprisoned for the possession of a catapult that fired teddy bears. The idea of Canada having political prisoners should cause an outrage,' said David Bannerjee, another member of the group." Monday May 7, 2001: *Bearly Able to Breathe* emailed News Release.

V What the Prime Minister Said

In Part V three themes are employed: the shamans' journey to Adlivun, an integral part of the Sedna legend; global corporate control, and the prolonged immiseration of vast numbers of Latin and South Americans.

310. Defining the nature and very possibility of authentic democracy in a post-national, post-industrial, corporatist world is one of the key challenges for the 21st century, as was recognized by the media-led discourse surrounding the summit. As *The Toronto Star* pointed out, "...[I]n Venezuela's case, representative democracy has been a trap that almost led the country to bloodshed," said [Hugo] Chavez.... "Some barons who were elected felt they had a blank cheque to rob, betray and steamroll others." *The Toronto Star* 23/04/01, A6. Letters to the editor of *The Toronto Star* on 23/04/01 by Luke Ploski and Resh Budhu stressed the questionable legitimacy of North American elections, given low voter turnout, and also, the fact that only through the collective agreement of the citizenry is legislative power transferred into the hands of a single governing body. Budhu emphasizes that "where government is subject to corruption or mismanagement, continual vigilance on the part of the population is an absolute necessity if the integrity of the system is to be maintained.... Where the summit seeks the creation of a global state, purely through economic imperatives, where is the voice of democracy in this meeting? It is out on the streets behind the barricades." As for the celebrated democracy clause itself, as Latin American specialist Paul Knox observed in a post-summit edition of *The Globe and Mail*, "the essential part of the clause is this: 'Any unconstitutional alteration or interruption of the democratic order in a state of the hemisphere constitutes an insurmountable obstacle to the participation of that state's government in the Summit of the Americas process....' There are huge questions about how the clause would work. Would shutting down a newspaper be enough to suspend a country's FTAA membership? How long will it be before we hear cries of a double standard, where poor, weak nations are held to a higher standard than major trading partners? Robin Rosenberg of the North-South Center at the University of Miami notes that whatever mechanism is adopted, the United States—as an OAS member—will have formal permission to pass judgment on Latin American countries' internal politics. 'The asymmetry of power is such that the United States can go in and say 'we want this,' and have leverage to do so—especially when they are taking 50 or 60 or 80 per cent of a country's exports,' he says." *The Globe and Mail*, 23/04/01 A17.

313. Media throughout the world have expressed alarm at the scandalous decline in Canada's methods of testing and regulating the condition of its drinking water. The outbreak of e coli contamination in Walkerton, Ontario in 2000, killed 7 people and made thousands of others severely ill. Some time later, the town of North Battleford, Saskatchewan, discovered its drinking water to be contaminated. An alarmingly high number of communities across Canada have been on alert to boil drinking water to prevent possible outbreaks of deadly diseases.

323. Reminiscent, perhaps of the fulmer's promises to Sedna, are the promises held out to sceptical citizens of the benefits of the FTAA "...increasing trade will alleviate poverty, enhance freedom and democracy, and raise the standard of living in countries in the hemisphere." *The Toronto Star* 23/04/01, A8. Citizens may continue to be sceptical of leaders making such golden promises; as Dr Bob Dickson points out in a letter to the editor of *The Toronto Star,* "Figures reveal that, despite an increase in world trade of 25 per cent from 1995 to 1998, the poorest 100 countries, comprising 10 per cent of our global population, share in only 0.5 per cent of world exports. This is critically important to developing nations because they have to fund over 90 per cent of their social service budgets with less than 10 per cent com-

ing from our assistance and aid programs. Therefore trade revenue is absolutely essential for these very poor countries. However, this is where the free trade proposal breaks down. What is equally essential to the well being of these disadvantaged nations are their own tariffs, which fund a tremendous amount of their crucial social programs. What we need is a true paradigm shift in the developed world. This would entail removing our tariffs and barriers to goods flowing from these heavily indebted poor countries and allowing their products to flow freely across our borders while keeping their tariff system relatively intact." 21/04/01, B7. Scepticism regarding golden promises is also appropriate closer to home, as Canadians concerned about the intersection of environmental protection and the pure-profit motive will be aware: "Prime Minister Jean Chrétien says he is pushing U.S. President George W. Bush to buy as much Canadian energy as possible as part of the Bush administration's plan to pool North American energy.... Gerry Scott of the David Suzuki Foundation of Vancouver said any move to expand energy sales to the U.S. would threaten the environment and make it tough for Canada to meet commitments to cut greenhouse gas emissions." *The Toronto Star*, 24/04/01, A6.

327. Sedna's severed finger joints, it is said, became the seals and whales. In dreams, shamans descend to her in Adlivun and comb her hair, which her mutilated hands cannot untangle. In return, Sedna sends the seals and whales back to where her people hunt; Sedna, the Inuit say, is always generous to those who ask her help in the accustomed way.

348. A propos market forces acting as a remedy for homelessness, an illuminating view is offered by Michael Shapcott: "The big problem, when it comes to housing and poverty, is that the market can't and won't respond to the needs of low-income households. Quite simply, they are too poor to merit any attention from corporate interests.... Hundreds of thousands of Canadians will experience homelessness this year, with children and families suffering the biggest increase in numbers. More than 2.2.million living in rental households are on the brink of homelessness and millions more are just a few steps away.... The role of government under free trade is to assist the private market, not meet the basic needs of real people." *The Globe and Mail*, 23/04/01, A 15. Shapcott, at the time, was a research associate at the University of Toronto's Centre for Urban and Community Studies, compiling a non-

governmental report to the United Nations on Canada's compliance with the Habitat Agenda and the Istanbul declaration.

359. *Ya basta!* Or *Enough, already!* is the rallying cry of the Chiapas rebels inspired by Subcommandante Marcos to demand social and economic justice for the indigenous people of Mexico.

360-78. *Médecins sans Frontières*, World Literacy and Amnesty International are only a handful of world-wide organizations acting in the interests of the public good and in defence of the rights of all human beings on this planet to dignity, justice and a measure of prosperity.

368-371. Marshall McLuhan's concept of the Global Village would seem to have severely compromised the solipsism endorsed by philosopher F.H. Bradley and so beloved of T.S. Eliot. One consequence of McLuhanism has been the obsolescence of what might be called the Czechoslovakia Response circa 1938, ie, that what hap-

pens in small, faraway countries where English isn't generally spoken is of no consequence to World Powers. There are, of course, ironic, not to mention tragic elements to this development: the public sees what the media make available to their eyes and screens; earthquakes, famines may be widely covered, but the African Aids pandemic and the devastating plight of Byelorussian children, victims of the fallout of the Chernobyl explosion, are banished to the Ultima Thule of our collective imagination and conscience. Human kind, as T.S. Eliot observed—though in a rather different context—cannot bear too much reality.

376. "In a world in which the Soviet Union simply vanished and Nelson Mandela is now the *retired* president of South Africa, who can say what change is impossible?" Rick Salutin, *The Globe and Mail*, 28/04/01, F5.

385. V. a quote from *Le Nouvel Observateur*, cited by *Le Journal de Québec*, 22/04/01, p. 17, regarding "Une crainte confirmée par le troublant dérapage verbal du premier ministre du Canada, Jean Chrétien, ravalant avec mépris les préoccupations de la société civile à un bla-bla-bla." Though Mr. Chrétien later appeared to ascribe some intellectual and moral substance to the protestors' concerns, the intelligibility or lack thereof of his rhetoric continued to pose problems. For example, what sense could be made of his post-summit statement, reported in *The Toronto Star*, 23/04/01, A8, that "We do not possess everything. We know we can make mistakes and when people are watching us, it is called democracy"?

386. Corporations, Rick Salutin reminds us, "need governments to wield armies and police forces, since free trade and globalization don't just happen. People resist them fiercely. And since no corporation can yet field its own army—the illegitimacy would be patent—they need the legitimacy of democratic credentials, which is why the democracy clause at this summit will be toothless but not meaningless. The more they suppress resistance to their form of globalization, the more they need the cover of people who can say they were democratically elected, now go away and shut up." Rick Salutin, *The Globe and Mail*, 28/04/01, F5.

393. "Advance, retreat...defend...rest...begin again." Words of advice and encouragement exchanged by protestors at Québec City during the Summit of the Americas.

BIOGRAPHIES

Janice Kulyk Keefer is the award-winning author of numerous books of poetry, fiction and non-fiction, including *The Paris-Napoli Express, Transfigurations, Travelling Ladies, Rest Harrow, White of the Lesser Angels, Marrying the Sea, Thieves*, and a memoir, *Honey and Ashes; Midnight Stroll* is her third book of poetry. She teaches English and Creative Writing at the University of Guelph.

Natalka Husar was born in 1951 in New Jersey to Ukrainian immigrant parents, and in 1973 she moved to Toronto, Canada. Catalogued travelling solo exhibitions include *Faces Facades* (1980); *Behind the Irony Curtain* (1986); *Milk and Blood* (1988); *True Confessions* (1991); *Black Sea Blue* (1995) and *Blond With Dark Roots* (2001). Her work is represented in numerous public collections including the Canada Council Art Bank, the Canadian Museum of Civilization, and the National Gallery of Canada.

Claire Weissman Wilks is a Canadian artist working in drawing, brush drawing, lithography, monoprinting, and sculpture in bronze and clay. Her works are in numerous private collections in Canada and abroad, and have been exhibited in the National Gallery of Canada, and in Toronto, Calgary, Stockholm, New York, Jerusalem, Venice, Rome, and Zagreb – where she is the only Canadian to have been given a one-woman retrospective in the State National Museum – and in Mexico City and Monterrey – where she represented Canada during a month-long celebration of the country's culture. Her works have been published in: *Drawings* (1975), *Two of Us Together: Each of Us Alone* (1982), *Tremors* (1983), *Hillmother* (1983), *I Know Not Why the Roses Bloom* (1987), and *In the White Hotel* (1990).

Goran Petkovski of Macedonia, now living in Canada, has spent the past ten years shooting and exhibiting documentary photography, and has published in a variety of magazines.

Contents

Exile Editions

info@exileeditions.com
www.ExileEditions.com

publishers of singular
fiction, poetry, drama, photography and art
since 1976